Property Inspection Checklist

PROPERTY DETAILS

I0506603

BEDROOMS

		1	2	3	4
Flooring	Carpet				
	Floorboards				
	Tiles				
	Stained				
	Scratched				
	Cracks				
Walls	Paint				
	Wallpaper				
	Cracks				
	Damp patches				
Windows	Flyscreens				
	Blinds				
	Curtains				
	Lockable				
Balcony					
Ensuite					
Built-in wardrobe					
Air conditioning					
Ceiling fan					
Gas outlet					
TV aerial outlet					
Phone line					
Smoke alarm					
Number of power points					
Dimensions (metres)		X	X	X	X

BATHROOMS

		1	2	3
Flooring	Tiles			
	Other			
	Cracks			
Walls	Tiles			
	Paint			
	Wallpaper			
	Cracks			
	Damp patches			
Windows	Flyscreens			
	Blinds			
	Curtains			
	Lockable			
Water pressure	High			
	Medium			
	Low			
Shower	Free standing			
	Over bath			
Bath				
Vanity				
Cupboards				
Towel rails				
Extraction fan				
Heater				
Toilet attached				
Number of power points				

NOTES

Checklist	Good	Average	Poor	Additional Notes
Outdoor Steps and sidewalk				
Outdoor Paint				
Driveway				
Outdoor Plantation				
Outdoor Entry Way				
Indoor Entry Way				
Doors				
Doors Fixtures				
Flooring				
Carpeting				
Windows				
Window Screens				
Window Fixtures				
Window Furnishings				
Ceilings				
Light Fixtures				
Staircases				
Indoor Paint				
Electrical Outlets and Fixtures				
Shelving				
Bedrooms				
Wardrobes and Closets				
Living Room (s)				
Dining Room (s)				
Dens (s)				
Study (s)				
Storage				
Fireplaces				
Bathroom Tiles				
Bathroom Faucets				

Notes:

_____

_____

_____

_____

Address _____ Price _____

Bedrooms _____ Bathrooms _____ Sq.Ft. _____

Lot Size: _____ Year Built _____ School District _____

Annual Tax _____

EXTERIOR

	Good	Average	Poor
View/Yard/Landscaping	☐	☐	☐
Trees	☐	☐	☐
Lawn (Front)	☐	☐	☐
Lawn (Back)	☐	☐	☐
Fences (condition)	☐	☐	☐
Landscaping (condition)	☐	☐	☐
Irrigation / Sprinkler	☐	☐	☐
	☐	☐	☐
House Type	☐	☐	☐
Exterior Siding	☐	☐	☐
Deck / Patio / Porch	☐	☐	☐
Garage	☐	☐	☐
Window / Doors	☐	☐	☐
Roof / Gutters	☐	☐	☐
Fencing	☐	☐	☐

HOME SYSTEMS

	Good	Average	Poor
Electrical	☐	☐	☐
Air Conditioning / Fans	☐	☐	☐
Heating	☐	☐	☐
Security	☐	☐	☐
Plumbing	☐	☐	☐
Intercom	☐	☐	☐

FEATURES

	Good	Average	Poor
Home Warranty	☐	☐	☐
Energy Saving Features	☐	☐	☐

INTERIOR

	Good	Average	Poor
Walls / Trim / Ceilings	☐	☐	☐
Flooring	☐	☐	☐
Stairs	☐	☐	☐
Storage	☐	☐	☐
Living Room	☐	☐	☐
Family Room	☐	☐	☐
Dining Room	☐	☐	☐

	Good	Average	Poor
Master Bedroom	☐	☐	☐
Bedroom 2	☐	☐	☐
Bedroom 3	☐	☐	☐
Bedroom 4	☐	☐	☐
Master Bathroom	☐	☐	☐
Bathroom 2	☐	☐	☐
Bathroom 3	☐	☐	☐
Bonus / Game Room	☐	☐	☐

	Good	Average	Poor
Kitchen	☐	☐	☐
Cabinets	☐	☐	☐
Countertop	☐	☐	☐
Counter Space	☐	☐	☐
Flooring	☐	☐	☐
Oven / Stove	☐	☐	☐
Microwave	☐	☐	☐
Layout	☐	☐	☐
Light Fixtures	☐	☐	☐
Backsplash	☐	☐	☐
Pantry	☐	☐	☐
Appliances	☐	☐	☐
Island	☐	☐	☐

	Good	Average	Poor
Basement	☐	☐	☐
Garage	☐	☐	☐

COMMUNITY

	Good	Average	Poor
Immediate Neighborhood	☐	☐	☐
Close to Employment	☐	☐	☐
Close to Shopping	☐	☐	☐
Close to Transportation	☐	☐	☐
Close to Schools / Daycare	☐	☐	☐
Close to Places of Worship	☐	☐	☐
Near Recreational Facilities	☐	☐	☐
Close to Airport	☐	☐	☐
Near Police and Fire Department	☐	☐	☐

Property Inspection Checklist

PROPERTY DETAILS

BEDROOMS		1	2	3	4
Flooring	Carpet				
	Floorboards				
	Tiles				
	Stained				
	Scratched				
	Cracks				
Walls	Paint				
	Wallpaper				
	Cracks				
	Damp patches				
Windows	Flyscreens				
	Blinds				
	Curtains				
	Lockable				
Balcony					
Ensuite					
Built-in wardrobe					
Air conditioning					
Ceiling fan					
Gas outlet					
TV aerial outlet					
Phone line					
Smoke alarm					
Number of power points					
Dimensions (metres)		x	x	x	x

BATHROOMS		1	2	3
Flooring	Tiles			
	Other			
	Cracks			
Walls	Tiles			
	Paint			
	Wallpaper			
	Cracks			
	Damp patches			
Windows	Flyscreens			
	Blinds			
	Curtains			
	Lockable			
Water pressure	High			
	Medium			
	Low			
Shower	Free standing			
	Over bath			
Bath				
Vanity				
Cupboards				
Towel rails				
Extraction fan				
Heater				
Toilet attached				
Number of power points				

NOTES

Checklist	Good	Average	Poor	Additional Notes
Outdoor Steps and sidewalk				
Outdoor Paint				
Driveway				
Outdoor Plantation				
Outdoor Entry Way				
Indoor Entry Way				
Doors				
Doors Fixtures				
Flooring				
Carpeting				
Windows				
Window Screens				
Window Fixtures				
Window Furnishings				
Ceilings				
Light Fixtures				
Staircases				
Indoor Paint				
Electrical Outlets and Fixtures				
Shelving				
Bedrooms				
Wardrobes and Closets				
Living Room (s)				
Dining Room (s)				
Dens (s)				
Study (s)				
Storage				
Fireplaces				
Bathroom Tiles				
Bathroom Faucets				

Notes:
_____
_____
_____
_____

Address _____ Price _____

Bedrooms _____ Bathrooms _____ Sq.Ft. _____

Lot Size: _____ Year Built _____ School District _____

Annual Tax _____

EXTERIOR

	Good	Average	Poor
View/Yard/Landscaping	☐	☐	☐
Trees	☐	☐	☐
Lawn (Front)	☐	☐	☐
Lawn (Back)	☐	☐	☐
Fences (condition)	☐	☐	☐
Landscaping (condition)	☐	☐	☐
Irrigation / Sprinkler	☐	☐	☐
	☐	☐	☐
House Type	☐	☐	☐
Exterior Siding	☐	☐	☐
Deck / Patio / Porch	☐	☐	☐
Garage	☐	☐	☐
Window / Doors	☐	☐	☐
Roof / Gutters	☐	☐	☐
Fencing	☐	☐	☐

HOME SYSTEMS

	Good	Average	Poor
Electrical	☐	☐	☐
Air Conditioning / Fans	☐	☐	☐
Heating	☐	☐	☐
Security	☐	☐	☐
Plumbing	☐	☐	☐
Intercom	☐	☐	☐

FEATURES

	Good	Average	Poor
Home Warranty	☐	☐	☐
Energy Saving Features	☐	☐	☐

INTERIOR

	Good	Average	Poor
Walls / Trim / Ceilings	☐	☐	☐
Flooring	☐	☐	☐
Stairs	☐	☐	☐
Storage	☐	☐	☐
Living Room	☐	☐	☐
Family Room	☐	☐	☐
Dining Room	☐	☐	☐

	Good	Average	Poor
Master Bedroom	☐	☐	☐
Bedroom 2	☐	☐	☐
Bedroom 3	☐	☐	☐
Bedroom 4	☐	☐	☐
Master Bathroom	☐	☐	☐
Bathroom 2	☐	☐	☐
Bathroom 3	☐	☐	☐
Bonus / Game Room	☐	☐	☐

	Good	Average	Poor
Kitchen			
Cabinets	☐	☐	☐
Countertop	☐	☐	☐
Counter Space	☐	☐	☐
Flooring	☐	☐	☐
Oven / Stove	☐	☐	☐
Microwave	☐	☐	☐
Layout	☐	☐	☐
Light Fixtures	☐	☐	☐
Backsplash	☐	☐	☐
Pantry	☐	☐	☐
Appliances	☐	☐	☐
Island	☐	☐	☐

	Good	Average	Poor
Basement	☐	☐	☐
Garage	☐	☐	☐

COMMUNITY

	Good	Average	Poor
Immediate Neighborhood	☐	☐	☐
Close to Employment	☐	☐	☐
Close to Shopping	☐	☐	☐
Close to Transportation	☐	☐	☐
Close to Schools / Daycare	☐	☐	☐
Close to Places of Worship	☐	☐	☐
Near Recreational Facilities	☐	☐	☐
Close to Airport	☐	☐	☐
Near Police and Fire Department	☐	☐	☐

Property Inspection Checklist

PROPERTY DETAILS

BEDROOMS		1	2	3	4
Flooring	Carpet				
	Floorboards				
	Tiles				
	Stained				
	Scratched				
	Cracks				
Walls	Paint				
	Wallpaper				
	Cracks				
	Damp patches				
Windows	Flyscreens				
	Blinds				
	Curtains				
	Lockable				
Balcony					
Ensuite					
Built-in wardrobe					
Air conditioning					
Ceiling fan					
Gas outlet					
TV aerial outlet					
Phone line					
Smoke alarm					
Number of power points					
Dimensions (metres)		x	x	x	x

BATHROOMS		1	2	3
Flooring	Tiles			
	Other			
	Cracks			
Walls	Tiles			
	Paint			
	Wallpaper			
	Cracks			
	Damp patches			
Windows	Flyscreens			
	Blinds			
	Curtains			
	Lockable			
Water pressure	High			
	Medium			
	Low			
Shower	Free standing			
	Over bath			
Bath				
Vanity				
Cupboards				
Towel rails				
Extraction fan				
Heater				
Toilet attached				
Number of power points				

NOTES

Checklist	Good	Average	Poor	Additional Notes
Outdoor Steps and sidewalk				
Outdoor Paint				
Driveway				
Outdoor Plantation				
Outdoor Entry Way				
Indoor Entry Way				
Doors				
Doors Fixtures				
Flooring				
Carpeting				
Windows				
Window Screens				
Window Fixtures				
Window Furnishings				
Ceilings				
Light Fixtures				
Staircases				
Indoor Paint				
Electrical Outlets and Fixtures				
Shelving				
Bedrooms				
Wardrobes and Closets				
Living Room (s)				
Dining Room (s)				
Dens (s)				
Study (s)				
Storage				
Fireplaces				
Bathroom Tiles				
Bathroom Faucets				

Notes:

_____

_____

_____

_____

Address _____   Price _____

Bedrooms _____   Bathrooms _____   Sq.Ft. _____

Lot Size: _____   Year Built _____   School District _____

Annual Tax _____

EXTERIOR

	Good	Average	Poor
View/Yard/Landscaping	☐	☐	☐
Trees	☐	☐	☐
Lawn (Front)	☐	☐	☐
Lawn (Back)	☐	☐	☐
Fences (condition)	☐	☐	☐
Landscaping (condition)	☐	☐	☐
Irrigation / Sprinkler	☐	☐	☐
House Type	☐	☐	☐
Exterior Siding	☐	☐	☐
Deck / Patio / Porch	☐	☐	☐
Garage	☐	☐	☐
Window / Doors	☐	☐	☐
Roof / Gutters	☐	☐	☐
Fencing	☐	☐	☐

HOME SYSTEMS

	Good	Average	Poor
Electrical	☐	☐	☐
Air Conditioning / Fans	☐	☐	☐
Heating	☐	☐	☐
Security	☐	☐	☐
Plumbing	☐	☐	☐
Intercom	☐	☐	☐

FEATURES

	Good	Average	Poor
Home Warranty	☐	☐	☐
Energy Saving Features	☐	☐	☐

INTERIOR

	Good	Average	Poor
Walls / Trim / Ceilings	☐	☐	☐
Flooring	☐	☐	☐
Stairs	☐	☐	☐
Storage	☐	☐	☐
Living Room	☐	☐	☐
Family Room	☐	☐	☐
Dining Room	☐	☐	☐

	Good	Average	Poor
Master Bedroom	☐	☐	☐
Bedroom 2	☐	☐	☐
Bedroom 3	☐	☐	☐
Bedroom 4	☐	☐	☐
Master Bathroom	☐	☐	☐
Bathroom 2	☐	☐	☐
Bathroom 3	☐	☐	☐
Bonus / Game Room	☐	☐	☐

Kitchen

	Good	Average	Poor
Cabinets	☐	☐	☐
Countertop	☐	☐	☐
Counter Space	☐	☐	☐
Flooring	☐	☐	☐
Oven / Stove	☐	☐	☐
Microwave	☐	☐	☐
Layout	☐	☐	☐
Light Fixtures	☐	☐	☐
Backsplash	☐	☐	☐
Pantry	☐	☐	☐
Appliances	☐	☐	☐
Island	☐	☐	☐

	Good	Average	Poor
Basement	☐	☐	☐
Garage	☐	☐	☐

COMMUNITY

	Good	Average	Poor
Immediate Neighborhood	☐	☐	☐
Close to Employment	☐	☐	☐
Close to Shopping	☐	☐	☐
Close to Transportation	☐	☐	☐
Close to Schools / Daycare	☐	☐	☐
Close to Places of Worship	☐	☐	☐
Near Recreational Facilities	☐	☐	☐
Close to Airport	☐	☐	☐
Near Police and Fire Department	☐	☐	☐

Property Inspection Checklist

PROPERTY DETAILS

BEDROOMS		1	2	3	4
Flooring	Carpet				
	Floorboards				
	Tiles				
	Stained				
	Scratched				
	Cracks				
Walls	Paint				
	Wallpaper				
	Cracks				
	Damp patches				
Windows	Flyscreens				
	Blinds				
	Curtains				
	Lockable				
Balcony					
Ensuite					
Built-in wardrobe					
Air conditioning					
Ceiling fan					
Gas outlet					
TV aerial outlet					
Phone line					
Smoke alarm					
Number of power points					
Dimensions (metres)		x	x	x	x

BATHROOMS		1	2	3
Flooring	Tiles			
	Other			
	Cracks			
Walls	Tiles			
	Paint			
	Wallpaper			
	Cracks			
	Damp patches			
Windows	Flyscreens			
	Blinds			
	Curtains			
	Lockable			
Water pressure	High			
	Medium			
	Low			
Shower	Free standing			
	Over bath			
Bath				
Vanity				
Cupboards				
Towel rails				
Extraction fan				
Heater				
Toilet attached				
Number of power points				

NOTES

Checklist	Good	Average	Poor	Additional Notes
Outdoor Steps and sidewalk				
Outdoor Paint				
Driveway				
Outdoor Plantation				
Outdoor Entry Way				
Indoor Entry Way				
Doors				
Doors Fixtures				
Flooring				
Carpeting				
Windows				
Window Screens				
Window Fixtures				
Window Furnishings				
Ceilings				
Light Fixtures				
Staircases				
Indoor Paint				
Electrical Outlets and Fixtures				
Shelving				
Bedrooms				
Wardrobes and Closets				
Living Room (s)				
Dining Room (s)				
Dens (s)				
Study (s)				
Storage				
Fireplaces				
Bathroom Tiles				
Bathroom Faucets				

Notes:

_____

_____

_____

_____

Address _____ Price _____

Bedrooms _____ Bathrooms _____ Sq.Ft. _____

Lot Size: _____ Year Built _____ School District _____

Annual Tax _____

EXTERIOR

	Good	Average	Poor
View/Yard/Landscaping	☐	☐	☐
Trees	☐	☐	☐
Lawn (Front)	☐	☐	☐
Lawn (Back)	☐	☐	☐
Fences (condition)	☐	☐	☐
Landscaping (condition)	☐	☐	☐
Irrigation / Sprinkler	☐	☐	☐
	☐	☐	☐
House Type	☐	☐	☐
Exterior Siding	☐	☐	☐
Deck / Patio / Porch	☐	☐	☐
Garage	☐	☐	☐
Window / Doors	☐	☐	☐
Roof / Gutters	☐	☐	☐
Fencing	☐	☐	☐

HOME SYSTEMS

	Good	Average	Poor
Electrical	☐	☐	☐
Air Conditioning / Fans	☐	☐	☐
Heating	☐	☐	☐
Security	☐	☐	☐
Plumbing	☐	☐	☐
Intercom	☐	☐	☐

FEATURES

	Good	Average	Poor
Home Warranty	☐	☐	☐
Energy Saving Features	☐	☐	☐

INTERIOR

	Good	Average	Poor
Walls / Trim / Ceilings	☐	☐	☐
Flooring	☐	☐	☐
Stairs	☐	☐	☐
Storage	☐	☐	☐
Living Room	☐	☐	☐
Family Room	☐	☐	☐
Dining Room	☐	☐	☐

	Good	Average	Poor
Master Bedroom	☐	☐	☐
Bedroom 2	☐	☐	☐
Bedroom 3	☐	☐	☐
Bedroom 4	☐	☐	☐
Master Bathroom	☐	☐	☐
Bathroom 2	☐	☐	☐
Bathroom 3	☐	☐	☐
Bonus / Game Room	☐	☐	☐

	Good	Average	Poor
Kitchen	☐	☐	☐
Cabinets	☐	☐	☐
Countertop	☐	☐	☐
Counter Space	☐	☐	☐
Flooring	☐	☐	☐
Oven / Stove	☐	☐	☐
Microwave	☐	☐	☐
Layout	☐	☐	☐
Light Fixtures	☐	☐	☐
Backsplash	☐	☐	☐
Pantry	☐	☐	☐
Appliances	☐	☐	☐
Island	☐	☐	☐

	Good	Average	Poor
Basement	☐	☐	☐
Garage	☐	☐	☐

COMMUNITY

	Good	Average	Poor
Immediate Neighborhood	☐	☐	☐
Close to Employment	☐	☐	☐
Close to Shopping	☐	☐	☐
Close to Transportation	☐	☐	☐
Close to Schools / Daycare	☐	☐	☐
Close to Places of Worship	☐	☐	☐
Near Recreational Facilities	☐	☐	☐
Close to Airport	☐	☐	☐
Near Police and Fire Department	☐	☐	☐

Property Inspection Checklist

PROPERTY DETAILS

BEDROOMS		1	2	3	4
Flooring	Carpet				
	Floorboards				
	Tiles				
	Stained				
	Scratched				
	Cracks				
Walls	Paint				
	Wallpaper				
	Cracks				
	Damp patches				
Windows	Flyscreens				
	Blinds				
	Curtains				
	Lockable				
Balcony					
Ensuite					
Built-in wardrobe					
Air conditioning					
Ceiling fan					
Gas outlet					
TV aerial outlet					
Phone line					
Smoke alarm					
Number of power points					
Dimensions (metres)		x	x	x	x

BATHROOMS		1	2	3
Flooring	Tiles			
	Other			
	Cracks			
Walls	Tiles			
	Paint			
	Wallpaper			
	Cracks			
	Damp patches			
Windows	Flyscreens			
	Blinds			
	Curtains			
	Lockable			
Water pressure	High			
	Medium			
	Low			
Shower	Free standing			
	Over bath			
Bath				
Vanity				
Cupboards				
Towel rails				
Extraction fan				
Heater				
Toilet attached				
Number of power points				

NOTES

Checklist	Good	Average	Poor	Additional Notes
Outdoor Steps and sidewalk				
Outdoor Paint				
Driveway				
Outdoor Plantation				
Outdoor Entry Way				
Indoor Entry Way				
Doors				
Doors Fixtures				
Flooring				
Carpeting				
Windows				
Window Screens				
Window Fixtures				
Window Furnishings				
Ceilings				
Light Fixtures				
Staircases				
Indoor Paint				
Electrical Outlets and Fixtures				
Shelving				
Bedrooms				
Wardrobes and Closets				
Living Room (s)				
Dining Room (s)				
Dens (s)				
Study (s)				
Storage				
Fireplaces				
Bathroom Tiles				
Bathroom Faucets				

Notes:

_____

_____

_____

_____

Address _____   Price _____

Bedrooms _____   Bathrooms _____   Sq.Ft. _____

Lot Size: _____   Year Built _____   School District _____

Annual Tax _____

EXTERIOR

	Good	Average	Poor
View/Yard/Landscaping	☐	☐	☐
Trees	☐	☐	☐
Lawn (Front)	☐	☐	☐
Lawn (Back)	☐	☐	☐
Fences (condition)	☐	☐	☐
Landscaping (condition)	☐	☐	☐
Irrigation / Sprinkler	☐	☐	☐
	☐	☐	☐
House Type	☐	☐	☐
Exterior Siding	☐	☐	☐
Deck / Patio / Porch	☐	☐	☐
Garage	☐	☐	☐
Window / Doors	☐	☐	☐
Roof / Gutters	☐	☐	☐
Fencing	☐	☐	☐

HOME SYSTEMS

	Good	Average	Poor
Electrical	☐	☐	☐
Air Conditioning / Fans	☐	☐	☐
Heating	☐	☐	☐
Security	☐	☐	☐
Plumbing	☐	☐	☐
Intercom	☐	☐	☐

FEATURES

	Good	Average	Poor
Home Warranty	☐	☐	☐
Energy Saving Features	☐	☐	☐

INTERIOR

	Good	Average	Poor
Walls / Trim / Ceilings	☐	☐	☐
Flooring	☐	☐	☐
Stairs	☐	☐	☐
Storage	☐	☐	☐
Living Room	☐	☐	☐
Family Room	☐	☐	☐
Dining Room	☐	☐	☐

	Good	Average	Poor
Master Bedroom	☐	☐	☐
Bedroom 2	☐	☐	☐
Bedroom 3	☐	☐	☐
Bedroom 4	☐	☐	☐
Master Bathroom	☐	☐	☐
Bathroom 2	☐	☐	☐
Bathroom 3	☐	☐	☐
Bonus / Game Room	☐	☐	☐

	Good	Average	Poor
Kitchen	☐	☐	☐
Cabinets	☐	☐	☐
Countertop	☐	☐	☐
Counter Space	☐	☐	☐
Flooring	☐	☐	☐
Oven / Stove	☐	☐	☐
Microwave	☐	☐	☐
Layout	☐	☐	☐
Light Fixtures	☐	☐	☐
Backsplash	☐	☐	☐
Pantry	☐	☐	☐
Appliances	☐	☐	☐
Island	☐	☐	☐

	Good	Average	Poor
Basement	☐	☐	☐
Garage	☐	☐	☐

COMMUNITY

	Good	Average	Poor
Immediate Neighborhood	☐	☐	☐
Close to Employment	☐	☐	☐
Close to Shopping	☐	☐	☐
Close to Transportation	☐	☐	☐
Close to Schools / Daycare	☐	☐	☐
Close to Places of Worship	☐	☐	☐
Near Recreational Facilities	☐	☐	☐
Close to Airport	☐	☐	☐
Near Police and Fire Department	☐	☐	☐

Property Inspection Checklist

PROPERTY DETAILS

BEDROOMS		1	2	3	4	BATHROOMS		1	2	3
Flooring	Carpet					Flooring	Tiles			
	Floorboards						Other			
	Tiles						Cracks			
	Stained					Walls	Tiles			
	Scratched						Paint			
	Cracks						Wallpaper			
Walls	Paint						Cracks			
	Wallpaper						Damp patches			
	Cracks					Windows	Flyscreens			
	Damp patches						Blinds			
Windows	Flyscreens						Curtains			
	Blinds						Lockable			
	Curtains					Water pressure	High			
	Lockable						Medium			
Balcony							Low			
Ensuite						Shower	Free standing			
Built-in wardrobe							Over bath			
Air conditioning						Bath				
Ceiling fan						Vanity				
Gas outlet						Cupboards				
TV aerial outlet						Towel rails				
Phone line						Extraction fan				
Smoke alarm						Heater				
Number of power points						Toilet attached				
Dimensions (metres)		x	x	x	x	Number of power points				

NOTES

Checklist	Good	Average	Poor	Additional Notes
Outdoor Steps and sidewalk				
Outdoor Paint				
Driveway				
Outdoor Plantation				
Outdoor Entry Way				
Indoor Entry Way				
Doors				
Doors Fixtures				
Flooring				
Carpeting				
Windows				
Window Screens				
Window Fixtures				
Window Furnishings				
Ceilings				
Light Fixtures				
Staircases				
Indoor Paint				
Electrical Outlets and Fixtures				
Shelving				
Bedrooms				
Wardrobes and Closets				
Living Room (s)				
Dining Room (s)				
Dens (s)				
Study (s)				
Storage				
Fireplaces				
Bathroom Tiles				
Bathroom Faucets				

Notes:
_____
_____
_____
_____

Address _____ Price _____

Bedrooms _____ Bathrooms _____ Sq.Ft. _____

Lot Size: _____ Year Built _____ School District _____

Annual Tax _____

EXTERIOR

	Good	Average	Poor
View/Yard/Landscaping	☐	☐	☐
Trees	☐	☐	☐
Lawn (Front)	☐	☐	☐
Lawn (Back)	☐	☐	☐
Fences (condition)	☐	☐	☐
Landscaping (condition)	☐	☐	☐
Irrigation / Sprinkler	☐	☐	☐
	☐	☐	☐
House Type	☐	☐	☐
Exterior Siding	☐	☐	☐
Deck / Patio / Porch	☐	☐	☐
Garage	☐	☐	☐
Window / Doors	☐	☐	☐
Roof / Gutters	☐	☐	☐
Fencing	☐	☐	☐

HOME SYSTEMS

	Good	Average	Poor
Electrical	☐	☐	☐
Air Conditioning / Fans	☐	☐	☐
Heating	☐	☐	☐
Security	☐	☐	☐
Plumbing	☐	☐	☐
Intercom	☐	☐	☐

FEATURES

	Good	Average	Poor
Home Warranty	☐	☐	☐
Energy Saving Features	☐	☐	☐

INTERIOR

	Good	Average	Poor
Walls / Trim / Ceilings	☐	☐	☐
Flooring	☐	☐	☐
Stairs	☐	☐	☐
Storage	☐	☐	☐
Living Room	☐	☐	☐
Family Room	☐	☐	☐
Dining Room	☐	☐	☐

	Good	Average	Poor
Master Bedroom	☐	☐	☐
Bedroom 2	☐	☐	☐
Bedroom 3	☐	☐	☐
Bedroom 4	☐	☐	☐
Master Bathroom	☐	☐	☐
Bathroom 2	☐	☐	☐
Bathroom 3	☐	☐	☐
Bonus / Game Room	☐	☐	☐

	Good	Average	Poor
Kitchen	☐	☐	☐
Cabinets	☐	☐	☐
Countertop	☐	☐	☐
Counter Space	☐	☐	☐
Flooring	☐	☐	☐
Oven / Stove	☐	☐	☐
Microwave	☐	☐	☐
Layout	☐	☐	☐
Light Fixtures	☐	☐	☐
Backsplash	☐	☐	☐
Pantry	☐	☐	☐
Appliances	☐	☐	☐
Island	☐	☐	☐

	Good	Average	Poor
Basement	☐	☐	☐
Garage	☐	☐	☐

COMMUNITY

	Good	Average	Poor
Immediate Neighborhood	☐	☐	☐
Close to Employment	☐	☐	☐
Close to Shopping	☐	☐	☐
Close to Transportation	☐	☐	☐
Close to Schools / Daycare	☐	☐	☐
Close to Places of Worship	☐	☐	☐
Near Recreational Facilities	☐	☐	☐
Close to Airport	☐	☐	☐
Near Police and Fire Department	☐	☐	☐

Property Inspection Checklist

PROPERTY DETAILS

BEDROOMS		1	2	3	4
Flooring	Carpet				
	Floorboards				
	Tiles				
	Stained				
	Scratched				
	Cracks				
Walls	Paint				
	Wallpaper				
	Cracks				
	Damp patches				
Windows	Flyscreens				
	Blinds				
	Curtains				
	Lockable				
Balcony					
Ensuite					
Built-in wardrobe					
Air conditioning					
Ceiling fan					
Gas outlet					
TV aerial outlet					
Phone line					
Smoke alarm					
Number of power points					
Dimensions (metres)		x	x	x	x

BATHROOMS		1	2	3
Flooring	Tiles			
	Other			
	Cracks			
Walls	Tiles			
	Paint			
	Wallpaper			
	Cracks			
	Damp patches			
Windows	Flyscreens			
	Blinds			
	Curtains			
	Lockable			
Water pressure	High			
	Medium			
	Low			
Shower	Free standing			
	Over bath			
Bath				
Vanity				
Cupboards				
Towel rails				
Extraction fan				
Heater				
Toilet attached				
Number of power points				

NOTES

Checklist	Good	Average	Poor	Additional Notes
Outdoor Steps and sidewalk				
Outdoor Paint				
Driveway				
Outdoor Plantation				
Outdoor Entry Way				
Indoor Entry Way				
Doors				
Doors Fixtures				
Flooring				
Carpeting				
Windows				
Window Screens				
Window Fixtures				
Window Furnishings				
Ceilings				
Light Fixtures				
Staircases				
Indoor Paint				
Electrical Outlets and Fixtures				
Shelving				
Bedrooms				
Wardrobes and Closets				
Living Room (s)				
Dining Room (s)				
Dens (s)				
Study (s)				
Storage				
Fireplaces				
Bathroom Tiles				
Bathroom Faucets				

Notes:
_____
_____
_____
_____

Address _____   Price _____

Bedrooms _____   Bathrooms _____   Sq.Ft. _____

Lot Size: _____   Year Built _____   School District _____

Annual Tax _____

EXTERIOR

	Good	Average	Poor
View/Yard/Landscaping	☐	☐	☐
Trees	☐	☐	☐
Lawn (Front)	☐	☐	☐
Lawn (Back)	☐	☐	☐
Fences (condition)	☐	☐	☐
Landscaping (condition)	☐	☐	☐
Irrigation / Sprinkler	☐	☐	☐
House Type	☐	☐	☐
Exterior Siding	☐	☐	☐
Deck / Patio / Porch	☐	☐	☐
Garage	☐	☐	☐
Window / Doors	☐	☐	☐
Roof / Gutters	☐	☐	☐
Fencing	☐	☐	☐

HOME SYSTEMS

	Good	Average	Poor
Electrical	☐	☐	☐
Air Conditioning / Fans	☐	☐	☐
Heating	☐	☐	☐
Security	☐	☐	☐
Plumbing	☐	☐	☐
Intercom	☐	☐	☐

FEATURES

	Good	Average	Poor
Home Warranty	☐	☐	☐
Energy Saving Features	☐	☐	☐

INTERIOR

	Good	Average	Poor
Walls / Trim / Ceilings	☐	☐	☐
Flooring	☐	☐	☐
Stairs	☐	☐	☐
Storage	☐	☐	☐
Living Room	☐	☐	☐
Family Room	☐	☐	☐
Dining Room	☐	☐	☐

	Good	Average	Poor
Master Bedroom	☐	☐	☐
Bedroom 2	☐	☐	☐
Bedroom 3	☐	☐	☐
Bedroom 4	☐	☐	☐
Master Bathroom	☐	☐	☐
Bathroom 2	☐	☐	☐
Bathroom 3	☐	☐	☐
Bonus / Game Room	☐	☐	☐

Kitchen

	Good	Average	Poor
Cabinets	☐	☐	☐
Countertop	☐	☐	☐
Counter Space	☐	☐	☐
Flooring	☐	☐	☐
Oven / Stove	☐	☐	☐
Microwave	☐	☐	☐
Layout	☐	☐	☐
Light Fixtures	☐	☐	☐
Backsplash	☐	☐	☐
Pantry	☐	☐	☐
Appliances	☐	☐	☐
Island	☐	☐	☐

	Good	Average	Poor
Basement	☐	☐	☐
Garage	☐	☐	☐

COMMUNITY

	Good	Average	Poor
Immediate Neighborhood	☐	☐	☐
Close to Employment	☐	☐	☐
Close to Shopping	☐	☐	☐
Close to Transportation	☐	☐	☐
Close to Schools / Daycare	☐	☐	☐
Close to Places of Worship	☐	☐	☐
Near Recreational Facilities	☐	☐	☐
Close to Airport	☐	☐	☐
Near Police and Fire Department	☐	☐	☐

Property Inspection Checklist

PROPERTY DETAILS

BEDROOMS		1	2	3	4	BATHROOMS		1	2	3
Flooring	Carpet					Flooring	Tiles			
	Floorboards						Other			
	Tiles						Cracks			
	Stained					Walls	Tiles			
	Scratched						Paint			
	Cracks						Wallpaper			
Walls	Paint						Cracks			
	Wallpaper						Damp patches			
	Cracks					Windows	Flyscreens			
	Damp patches						Blinds			
Windows	Flyscreens						Curtains			
	Blinds						Lockable			
	Curtains					Water pressure	High			
	Lockable						Medium			
Balcony							Low			
Ensuite						Shower	Free standing			
Built-in wardrobe							Over bath			
Air conditioning						Bath				
Ceiling fan						Vanity				
Gas outlet						Cupboards				
TV aerial outlet						Towel rails				
Phone line						Extraction fan				
Smoke alarm						Heater				
Number of power points						Toilet attached				
Dimensions (metres)		x	x	x	x	Number of power points				

NOTES

Checklist	Good	Average	Poor	Additional Notes
Outdoor Steps and sidewalk				
Outdoor Paint				
Driveway				
Outdoor Plantation				
Outdoor Entry Way				
Indoor Entry Way				
Doors				
Doors Fixtures				
Flooring				
Carpeting				
Windows				
Window Screens				
Window Fixtures				
Window Furnishings				
Ceilings				
Light Fixtures				
Staircases				
Indoor Paint				
Electrical Outlets and Fixtures				
Shelving				
Bedrooms				
Wardrobes and Closets				
Living Room (s)				
Dining Room (s)				
Dens (s)				
Study (s)				
Storage				
Fireplaces				
Bathroom Tiles				
Bathroom Faucets				

Notes:
_____
_____
_____
_____
_____

Address _____ Price _____

Bedrooms _____ Bathrooms _____ Sq.Ft. _____

Lot Size: _____ Year Built _____ School District _____

Annual Tax _____

EXTERIOR

	Good	Average	Poor
View/Yard/Landscaping	☐	☐	☐
Trees	☐	☐	☐
Lawn (Front)	☐	☐	☐
Lawn (Back)	☐	☐	☐
Fences (condition)	☐	☐	☐
Landscaping (condition)	☐	☐	☐
Irrigation / Sprinkler	☐	☐	☐
House Type	☐	☐	☐
Exterior Siding	☐	☐	☐
Deck / Patio / Porch	☐	☐	☐
Garage	☐	☐	☐
Window / Doors	☐	☐	☐
Roof / Gutters	☐	☐	☐
Fencing	☐	☐	☐

HOME SYSTEMS

	Good	Average	Poor
Electrical	☐	☐	☐
Air Conditioning / Fans	☐	☐	☐
Heating	☐	☐	☐
Security	☐	☐	☐
Plumbing	☐	☐	☐
Intercom	☐	☐	☐

FEATURES

	Good	Average	Poor
Home Warranty	☐	☐	☐
Energy Saving Features	☐	☐	☐

INTERIOR

	Good	Average	Poor
Walls / Trim / Ceilings	☐	☐	☐
Flooring	☐	☐	☐
Stairs	☐	☐	☐
Storage	☐	☐	☐
Living Room	☐	☐	☐
Family Room	☐	☐	☐
Dining Room	☐	☐	☐

	Good	Average	Poor
Master Bedroom	☐	☐	☐
Bedroom 2	☐	☐	☐
Bedroom 3	☐	☐	☐
Bedroom 4	☐	☐	☐
Master Bathroom	☐	☐	☐
Bathroom 2	☐	☐	☐
Bathroom 3	☐	☐	☐
Bonus / Game Room	☐	☐	☐

	Good	Average	Poor
Kitchen	☐	☐	☐
Cabinets	☐	☐	☐
Countertop	☐	☐	☐
Counter Space	☐	☐	☐
Flooring	☐	☐	☐
Oven / Stove	☐	☐	☐
Microwave	☐	☐	☐
Layout	☐	☐	☐
Light Fixtures	☐	☐	☐
Backsplash	☐	☐	☐
Pantry	☐	☐	☐
Appliances	☐	☐	☐
Island	☐	☐	☐

	Good	Average	Poor
Basement	☐	☐	☐
Garage	☐	☐	☐

COMMUNITY

	Good	Average	Poor
Immediate Neighborhood	☐	☐	☐
Close to Employment	☐	☐	☐
Close to Shopping	☐	☐	☐
Close to Transportation	☐	☐	☐
Close to Schools / Daycare	☐	☐	☐
Close to Places of Worship	☐	☐	☐
Near Recreational Facilities	☐	☐	☐
Close to Airport	☐	☐	☐
Near Police and Fire Department	☐	☐	☐

Property Inspection Checklist

PROPERTY DETAILS

BEDROOMS		1	2	3	4
Flooring	Carpet				
	Floorboards				
	Tiles				
	Stained				
	Scratched				
	Cracks				
Walls	Paint				
	Wallpaper				
	Cracks				
	Damp patches				
Windows	Flyscreens				
	Blinds				
	Curtains				
	Lockable				
Balcony					
Ensuite					
Built-in wardrobe					
Air conditioning					
Ceiling fan					
Gas outlet					
TV aerial outlet					
Phone line					
Smoke alarm					
Number of power points					
Dimensions (metres)		X	X	X	X

BATHROOMS		1	2	3
Flooring	Tiles			
	Other			
	Cracks			
Walls	Tiles			
	Paint			
	Wallpaper			
	Cracks			
	Damp patches			
Windows	Flyscreens			
	Blinds			
	Curtains			
	Lockable			
Water pressure	High			
	Medium			
	Low			
Shower	Free standing			
	Over bath			
Bath				
Vanity				
Cupboards				
Towel rails				
Extraction fan				
Heater				
Toilet attached				
Number of power points				

NOTES

Checklist	Good	Average	Poor	Additional Notes
Outdoor Steps and sidewalk				
Outdoor Paint				
Driveway				
Outdoor Plantation				
Outdoor Entry Way				
Indoor Entry Way				
Doors				
Doors Fixtures				
Flooring				
Carpeting				
Windows				
Window Screens				
Window Fixtures				
Window Furnishings				
Ceilings				
Light Fixtures				
Staircases				
Indoor Paint				
Electrical Outlets and Fixtures				
Shelving				
Bedrooms				
Wardrobes and Closets				
Living Room (s)				
Dining Room (s)				
Dens (s)				
Study (s)				
Storage				
Fireplaces				
Bathroom Tiles				
Bathroom Faucets				

Notes:
_____
_____
_____
_____
_____

Address _____ Price _____

Bedrooms _____ Bathrooms _____ Sq.Ft. _____

Lot Size: _____ Year Built _____ School District _____

Annual Tax _____

EXTERIOR

	Good	Average	Poor
View/Yard/Landscaping	☐	☐	☐
Trees	☐	☐	☐
Lawn (Front)	☐	☐	☐
Lawn (Back)	☐	☐	☐
Fences (condition)	☐	☐	☐
Landscaping (condition)	☐	☐	☐
Irrigation / Sprinkler	☐	☐	☐
	☐	☐	☐
House Type	☐	☐	☐
Exterior Siding	☐	☐	☐
Deck / Patio / Porch	☐	☐	☐
Garage	☐	☐	☐
Window / Doors	☐	☐	☐
Roof / Gutters	☐	☐	☐
Fencing	☐	☐	☐

HOME SYSTEMS

	Good	Average	Poor
Electrical	☐	☐	☐
Air Conditioning / Fans	☐	☐	☐
Heating	☐	☐	☐
Security	☐	☐	☐
Plumbing	☐	☐	☐
Intercom	☐	☐	☐

FEATURES

	Good	Average	Poor
Home Warranty	☐	☐	☐
Energy Saving Features	☐	☐	☐

INTERIOR

	Good	Average	Poor
Walls / Trim / Ceilings	☐	☐	☐
Flooring	☐	☐	☐
Stairs	☐	☐	☐
Storage	☐	☐	☐
Living Room	☐	☐	☐
Family Room	☐	☐	☐
Dining Room	☐	☐	☐

	Good	Average	Poor
Master Bedroom	☐	☐	☐
Bedroom 2	☐	☐	☐
Bedroom 3	☐	☐	☐
Bedroom 4	☐	☐	☐
Master Bathroom	☐	☐	☐
Bathroom 2	☐	☐	☐
Bathroom 3	☐	☐	☐
Bonus / Game Room	☐	☐	☐

	Good	Average	Poor
Kitchen	☐	☐	☐
Cabinets	☐	☐	☐
Countertop	☐	☐	☐
Counter Space	☐	☐	☐
Flooring	☐	☐	☐
Oven / Stove	☐	☐	☐
Microwave	☐	☐	☐
Layout	☐	☐	☐
Light Fixtures	☐	☐	☐
Backsplash	☐	☐	☐
Pantry	☐	☐	☐
Appliances	☐	☐	☐
Island	☐	☐	☐

	Good	Average	Poor
Basement	☐	☐	☐
Garage	☐	☐	☐

COMMUNITY

	Good	Average	Poor
Immediate Neighborhood	☐	☐	☐
Close to Employment	☐	☐	☐
Close to Shopping	☐	☐	☐
Close to Transportation	☐	☐	☐
Close to Schools / Daycare	☐	☐	☐
Close to Places of Worship	☐	☐	☐
Near Recreational Facilities	☐	☐	☐
Close to Airport	☐	☐	☐
Near Police and Fire Department	☐	☐	☐

Property Inspection Checklist

PROPERTY DETAILS

BEDROOMS		1	2	3	4
Flooring	Carpet				
	Floorboards				
	Tiles				
	Stained				
	Scratched				
	Cracks				
Walls	Paint				
	Wallpaper				
	Cracks				
	Damp patches				
Windows	Flyscreens				
	Blinds				
	Curtains				
	Lockable				
Balcony					
Ensuite					
Built-in wardrobe					
Air conditioning					
Ceiling fan					
Gas outlet					
TV aerial outlet					
Phone line					
Smoke alarm					
Number of power points					
Dimensions (metres)		x	x	x	x

BATHROOMS		1	2	3
Flooring	Tiles			
	Other			
	Cracks			
Walls	Tiles			
	Paint			
	Wallpaper			
	Cracks			
	Damp patches			
Windows	Flyscreens			
	Blinds			
	Curtains			
	Lockable			
Water pressure	High			
	Medium			
	Low			
Shower	Free standing			
	Over bath			
Bath				
Vanity				
Cupboards				
Towel rails				
Extraction fan				
Heater				
Toilet attached				
Number of power points				

NOTES

Checklist	Good	Average	Poor	Additional Notes
Outdoor Steps and sidewalk				
Outdoor Paint				
Driveway				
Outdoor Plantation				
Outdoor Entry Way				
Indoor Entry Way				
Doors				
Doors Fixtures				
Flooring				
Carpeting				
Windows				
Window Screens				
Window Fixtures				
Window Furnishings				
Ceilings				
Light Fixtures				
Staircases				
Indoor Paint				
Electrical Outlets and Fixtures				
Shelving				
Bedrooms				
Wardrobes and Closets				
Living Room (s)				
Dining Room (s)				
Dens (s)				
Study (s)				
Storage				
Fireplaces				
Bathroom Tiles				
Bathroom Faucets				

Notes:

_____

_____

_____

_____

Address _____ Price _____

Bedrooms _____ Bathrooms _____ Sq.Ft. _____

Lot Size: _____ Year Built _____ School District _____

Annual Tax _____

EXTERIOR

	Good	Average	Poor
View/Yard/Landscaping	☐	☐	☐
Trees	☐	☐	☐
Lawn (Front)	☐	☐	☐
Lawn (Back)	☐	☐	☐
Fences (condition)	☐	☐	☐
Landscaping (condition)	☐	☐	☐
Irrigation / Sprinkler	☐	☐	☐
	☐	☐	☐
House Type	☐	☐	☐
Exterior Siding	☐	☐	☐
Deck / Patio / Porch	☐	☐	☐
Garage	☐	☐	☐
Window / Doors	☐	☐	☐
Roof / Gutters	☐	☐	☐
Fencing	☐	☐	☐

HOME SYSTEMS

	Good	Average	Poor
Electrical	☐	☐	☐
Air Conditioning / Fans	☐	☐	☐
Heating	☐	☐	☐
Security	☐	☐	☐
Plumbing	☐	☐	☐
Intercom	☐	☐	☐

FEATURES

	Good	Average	Poor
Home Warranty	☐	☐	☐
Energy Saving Features	☐	☐	☐

INTERIOR

	Good	Average	Poor
Walls / Trim / Ceilings	☐	☐	☐
Flooring	☐	☐	☐
Stairs	☐	☐	☐
Storage	☐	☐	☐
Living Room	☐	☐	☐
Family Room	☐	☐	☐
Dining Room	☐	☐	☐

	Good	Average	Poor
Master Bedroom	☐	☐	☐
Bedroom 2	☐	☐	☐
Bedroom 3	☐	☐	☐
Bedroom 4	☐	☐	☐
Master Bathroom	☐	☐	☐
Bathroom 2	☐	☐	☐
Bathroom 3	☐	☐	☐
Bonus / Game Room	☐	☐	☐

	Good	Average	Poor
Kitchen	☐	☐	☐
Cabinets	☐	☐	☐
Countertop	☐	☐	☐
Counter Space	☐	☐	☐
Flooring	☐	☐	☐
Oven / Stove	☐	☐	☐
Microwave	☐	☐	☐
Layout	☐	☐	☐
Light Fixtures	☐	☐	☐
Backsplash	☐	☐	☐
Pantry	☐	☐	☐
Appliances	☐	☐	☐
Island	☐	☐	☐

	Good	Average	Poor
Basement	☐	☐	☐
Garage	☐	☐	☐

COMMUNITY

	Good	Average	Poor
Immediate Neighborhood	☐	☐	☐
Close to Employment	☐	☐	☐
Close to Shopping	☐	☐	☐
Close to Transportation	☐	☐	☐
Close to Schools / Daycare	☐	☐	☐
Close to Places of Worship	☐	☐	☐
Near Recreational Facilities	☐	☐	☐
Close to Airport	☐	☐	☐
Near Police and Fire Department	☐	☐	☐

Property Inspection Checklist

PROPERTY DETAILS

BEDROOMS

		1	2	3	4
Flooring	Carpet				
	Floorboards				
	Tiles				
	Stained				
	Scratched				
	Cracks				
Walls	Paint				
	Wallpaper				
	Cracks				
	Damp patches				
Windows	Flyscreens				
	Blinds				
	Curtains				
	Lockable				
Balcony					
Ensuite					
Built-in wardrobe					
Air conditioning					
Ceiling fan					
Gas outlet					
TV aerial outlet					
Phone line					
Smoke alarm					
Number of power points					
Dimensions (metres)		x	x	x	x

BATHROOMS

		1	2	3
Flooring	Tiles			
	Other			
	Cracks			
Walls	Tiles			
	Paint			
	Wallpaper			
	Cracks			
	Damp patches			
Windows	Flyscreens			
	Blinds			
	Curtains			
	Lockable			
Water pressure	High			
	Medium			
	Low			
Shower	Free standing			
	Over bath			
Bath				
Vanity				
Cupboards				
Towel rails				
Extraction fan				
Heater				
Toilet attached				
Number of power points				

NOTES

Checklist	Good	Average	Poor	Additional Notes
Outdoor Steps and sidewalk				
Outdoor Paint				
Driveway				
Outdoor Plantation				
Outdoor Entry Way				
Indoor Entry Way				
Doors				
Doors Fixtures				
Flooring				
Carpeting				
Windows				
Window Screens				
Window Fixtures				
Window Furnishings				
Ceilings				
Light Fixtures				
Staircases				
Indoor Paint				
Electrical Outlets and Fixtures				
Shelving				
Bedrooms				
Wardrobes and Closets				
Living Room (s)				
Dining Room (s)				
Dens (s)				
Study (s)				
Storage				
Fireplaces				
Bathroom Tiles				
Bathroom Faucets				

Notes:

_____

_____

_____

_____

Address _____ Price _____

Bedrooms _____ Bathrooms _____ Sq.Ft. _____

Lot Size: _____ Year Built _____ School District _____

Annual Tax _____

EXTERIOR

	Good	Average	Poor
View/Yard/Landscaping	☐	☐	☐
Trees	☐	☐	☐
Lawn (Front)	☐	☐	☐
Lawn (Back)	☐	☐	☐
Fences (condition)	☐	☐	☐
Landscaping (condition)	☐	☐	☐
Irrigation / Sprinkler	☐	☐	☐
	☐	☐	☐
House Type	☐	☐	☐
Exterior Siding	☐	☐	☐
Deck / Patio / Porch	☐	☐	☐
Garage	☐	☐	☐
Window / Doors	☐	☐	☐
Roof / Gutters	☐	☐	☐
Fencing	☐	☐	☐

HOME SYSTEMS

	Good	Average	Poor
Electrical	☐	☐	☐
Air Conditioning / Fans	☐	☐	☐
Heating	☐	☐	☐
Security	☐	☐	☐
Plumbing	☐	☐	☐
Intercom	☐	☐	☐

FEATURES

	Good	Average	Poor
Home Warranty	☐	☐	☐
Energy Saving Features	☐	☐	☐

INTERIOR

	Good	Average	Poor
Walls / Trim / Ceilings	☐	☐	☐
Flooring	☐	☐	☐
Stairs	☐	☐	☐
Storage	☐	☐	☐
Living Room	☐	☐	☐
Family Room	☐	☐	☐
Dining Room	☐	☐	☐

	Good	Average	Poor
Master Bedroom	☐	☐	☐
Bedroom 2	☐	☐	☐
Bedroom 3	☐	☐	☐
Bedroom 4	☐	☐	☐
Master Bathroom	☐	☐	☐
Bathroom 2	☐	☐	☐
Bathroom 3	☐	☐	☐
Bonus / Game Room	☐	☐	☐

	Good	Average	Poor
Kitchen	☐	☐	☐
Cabinets	☐	☐	☐
Countertop	☐	☐	☐
Counter Space	☐	☐	☐
Flooring	☐	☐	☐
Oven / Stove	☐	☐	☐
Microwave	☐	☐	☐
Layout	☐	☐	☐
Light Fixtures	☐	☐	☐
Backsplash	☐	☐	☐
Pantry	☐	☐	☐
Appliances	☐	☐	☐
Island	☐	☐	☐

	Good	Average	Poor
Basement	☐	☐	☐
Garage	☐	☐	☐

COMMUNITY

	Good	Average	Poor
Immediate Neighborhood	☐	☐	☐
Close to Employment	☐	☐	☐
Close to Shopping	☐	☐	☐
Close to Transportation	☐	☐	☐
Close to Schools / Daycare	☐	☐	☐
Close to Places of Worship	☐	☐	☐
Near Recreational Facilities	☐	☐	☐
Close to Airport	☐	☐	☐
Near Police and Fire Department	☐	☐	☐

Property Inspection Checklist

PROPERTY DETAILS

BEDROOMS		1	2	3	4	BATHROOMS		1	2	3
Flooring	Carpet					Flooring	Tiles			
	Floorboards						Other			
	Tiles						Cracks			
	Stained					Walls	Tiles			
	Scratched						Paint			
	Cracks						Wallpaper			
Walls	Paint						Cracks			
	Wallpaper						Damp patches			
	Cracks					Windows	Flyscreens			
	Damp patches						Blinds			
Windows	Flyscreens						Curtains			
	Blinds						Lockable			
	Curtains					Water pressure	High			
	Lockable						Medium			
Balcony							Low			
Ensuite						Shower	Free standing			
Built-in wardrobe							Over bath			
Air conditioning						Bath				
Ceiling fan						Vanity				
Gas outlet						Cupboards				
TV aerial outlet						Towel rails				
Phone line						Extraction fan				
Smoke alarm						Heater				
Number of power points						Toilet attached				
Dimensions (metres)		x	x	x	x	Number of power points				

NOTES

Checklist	Good	Average	Poor	Additional Notes
Outdoor Steps and sidewalk				
Outdoor Paint				
Driveway				
Outdoor Plantation				
Outdoor Entry Way				
Indoor Entry Way				
Doors				
Doors Fixtures				
Flooring				
Carpeting				
Windows				
Window Screens				
Window Fixtures				
Window Furnishings				
Ceilings				
Light Fixtures				
Staircases				
Indoor Paint				
Electrical Outlets and Fixtures				
Shelving				
Bedrooms				
Wardrobes and Closets				
Living Room (s)				
Dining Room (s)				
Dens (s)				
Study (s)				
Storage				
Fireplaces				
Bathroom Tiles				
Bathroom Faucets				

Notes:

_____

_____

_____

_____

Address _____ Price _____

Bedrooms _____ Bathrooms _____ Sq.Ft. _____

Lot Size: _____ Year Built _____ School District _____

Annual Tax _____

EXTERIOR

	Good	Average	Poor
View/Yard/Landscaping	☐	☐	☐
Trees	☐	☐	☐
Lawn (Front)	☐	☐	☐
Lawn (Back)	☐	☐	☐
Fences (condition)	☐	☐	☐
Landscaping (condition)	☐	☐	☐
Irrigation / Sprinkler	☐	☐	☐
	☐	☐	☐
House Type	☐	☐	☐
Exterior Siding	☐	☐	☐
Deck / Patio / Porch	☐	☐	☐
Garage	☐	☐	☐
Window / Doors	☐	☐	☐
Roof / Gutters	☐	☐	☐
Fencing	☐	☐	☐

HOME SYSTEMS

	Good	Average	Poor
Electrical	☐	☐	☐
Air Conditioning / Fans	☐	☐	☐
Heating	☐	☐	☐
Security	☐	☐	☐
Plumbing	☐	☐	☐
Intercom	☐	☐	☐

FEATURES

	Good	Average	Poor
Home Warranty	☐	☐	☐
Energy Saving Features	☐	☐	☐

INTERIOR

	Good	Average	Poor
Walls / Trim / Ceilings	☐	☐	☐
Flooring	☐	☐	☐
Stairs	☐	☐	☐
Storage	☐	☐	☐
Living Room	☐	☐	☐
Family Room	☐	☐	☐
Dining Room	☐	☐	☐

	Good	Average	Poor
Master Bedroom	☐	☐	☐
Bedroom 2	☐	☐	☐
Bedroom 3	☐	☐	☐
Bedroom 4	☐	☐	☐
Master Bathroom	☐	☐	☐
Bathroom 2	☐	☐	☐
Bathroom 3	☐	☐	☐
Bonus / Game Room	☐	☐	☐

	Good	Average	Poor
Kitchen	☐	☐	☐
Cabinets	☐	☐	☐
Countertop	☐	☐	☐
Counter Space	☐	☐	☐
Flooring	☐	☐	☐
Oven / Stove	☐	☐	☐
Microwave	☐	☐	☐
Layout	☐	☐	☐
Light Fixtures	☐	☐	☐
Backsplash	☐	☐	☐
Pantry	☐	☐	☐
Appliances	☐	☐	☐
Island	☐	☐	☐

	Good	Average	Poor
Basement	☐	☐	☐
Garage	☐	☐	☐

COMMUNITY

	Good	Average	Poor
Immediate Neighborhood	☐	☐	☐
Close to Employment	☐	☐	☐
Close to Shopping	☐	☐	☐
Close to Transportation	☐	☐	☐
Close to Schools / Daycare	☐	☐	☐
Close to Places of Worship	☐	☐	☐
Near Recreational Facilities	☐	☐	☐
Close to Airport	☐	☐	☐
Near Police and Fire Department	☐	☐	☐

Property Inspection Checklist

PROPERTY DETAILS

BEDROOMS		1	2	3	4
Flooring	Carpet				
	Floorboards				
	Tiles				
	Stained				
	Scratched				
	Cracks				
Walls	Paint				
	Wallpaper				
	Cracks				
	Damp patches				
Windows	Flyscreens				
	Blinds				
	Curtains				
	Lockable				
Balcony					
Ensuite					
Built-in wardrobe					
Air conditioning					
Ceiling fan					
Gas outlet					
TV aerial outlet					
Phone line					
Smoke alarm					
Number of power points					
Dimensions (metres)		X	X	X	X

BATHROOMS		1	2	3
Flooring	Tiles			
	Other			
	Cracks			
Walls	Tiles			
	Paint			
	Wallpaper			
	Cracks			
	Damp patches			
Windows	Flyscreens			
	Blinds			
	Curtains			
	Lockable			
Water pressure	High			
	Medium			
	Low			
Shower	Free standing			
	Over bath			
Bath				
Vanity				
Cupboards				
Towel rails				
Extraction fan				
Heater				
Toilet attached				
Number of power points				

NOTES

Checklist	Good	Average	Poor	Additional Notes
Outdoor Steps and sidewalk				
Outdoor Paint				
Driveway				
Outdoor Plantation				
Outdoor Entry Way				
Indoor Entry Way				
Doors				
Doors Fixtures				
Flooring				
Carpeting				
Windows				
Window Screens				
Window Fixtures				
Window Furnishings				
Ceilings				
Light Fixtures				
Staircases				
Indoor Paint				
Electrical Outlets and Fixtures				
Shelving				
Bedrooms				
Wardrobes and Closets				
Living Room (s)				
Dining Room (s)				
Dens (s)				
Study (s)				
Storage				
Fireplaces				
Bathroom Tiles				
Bathroom Faucets				

Notes:

_____

_____

_____

_____

Address _____   Price _____

Bedrooms _____   Bathrooms _____   Sq.Ft. _____

Lot Size: _____   Year Built _____   School District _____

Annual Tax _____

EXTERIOR

	Good	Average	Poor
View/Yard/Landscaping	☐	☐	☐
Trees	☐	☐	☐
Lawn (Front)	☐	☐	☐
Lawn (Back)	☐	☐	☐
Fences (condition)	☐	☐	☐
Landscaping (condition)	☐	☐	☐
Irrigation / Sprinkler	☐	☐	☐
	☐	☐	☐
House Type	☐	☐	☐
Exterior Siding	☐	☐	☐
Deck / Patio / Porch	☐	☐	☐
Garage	☐	☐	☐
Window / Doors	☐	☐	☐
Roof / Gutters	☐	☐	☐
Fencing	☐	☐	☐

HOME SYSTEMS

	Good	Average	Poor
Electrical	☐	☐	☐
Air Conditioning / Fans	☐	☐	☐
Heating	☐	☐	☐
Security	☐	☐	☐
Plumbing	☐	☐	☐
Intercom	☐	☐	☐

FEATURES

	Good	Average	Poor
Home Warranty	☐	☐	☐
Energy Saving Features	☐	☐	☐

INTERIOR

	Good	Average	Poor
Walls / Trim / Ceilings	☐	☐	☐
Flooring	☐	☐	☐
Stairs	☐	☐	☐
Storage	☐	☐	☐
Living Room	☐	☐	☐
Family Room	☐	☐	☐
Dining Room	☐	☐	☐

	Good	Average	Poor
Master Bedroom	☐	☐	☐
Bedroom 2	☐	☐	☐
Bedroom 3	☐	☐	☐
Bedroom 4	☐	☐	☐
Master Bathroom	☐	☐	☐
Bathroom 2	☐	☐	☐
Bathroom 3	☐	☐	☐
Bonus / Game Room	☐	☐	☐

	Good	Average	Poor
Kitchen	☐	☐	☐
Cabinets	☐	☐	☐
Countertop	☐	☐	☐
Counter Space	☐	☐	☐
Flooring	☐	☐	☐
Oven / Stove	☐	☐	☐
Microwave	☐	☐	☐
Layout	☐	☐	☐
Light Fixtures	☐	☐	☐
Backsplash	☐	☐	☐
Pantry	☐	☐	☐
Appliances	☐	☐	☐
Island	☐	☐	☐

	Good	Average	Poor
Basement	☐	☐	☐
Garage	☐	☐	☐

COMMUNITY

	Good	Average	Poor
Immediate Neighborhood	☐	☐	☐
Close to Employment	☐	☐	☐
Close to Shopping	☐	☐	☐
Close to Transportation	☐	☐	☐
Close to Schools / Daycare	☐	☐	☐
Close to Places of Worship	☐	☐	☐
Near Recreational Facilities	☐	☐	☐
Close to Airport	☐	☐	☐
Near Police and Fire Department	☐	☐	☐

Property Inspection Checklist

PROPERTY DETAILS

BEDROOMS		1	2	3	4
Flooring	Carpet				
	Floorboards				
	Tiles				
	Stained				
	Scratched				
	Cracks				
Walls	Paint				
	Wallpaper				
	Cracks				
	Damp patches				
Windows	Flyscreens				
	Blinds				
	Curtains				
	Lockable				
Balcony					
Ensuite					
Built-in wardrobe					
Air conditioning					
Ceiling fan					
Gas outlet					
TV aerial outlet					
Phone line					
Smoke alarm					
Number of power points					
Dimensions (metres)		x	x	x	x

BATHROOMS		1	2	3
Flooring	Tiles			
	Other			
	Cracks			
Walls	Tiles			
	Paint			
	Wallpaper			
	Cracks			
	Damp patches			
Windows	Flyscreens			
	Blinds			
	Curtains			
	Lockable			
Water pressure	High			
	Medium			
	Low			
Shower	Free standing			
	Over bath			
Bath				
Vanity				
Cupboards				
Towel rails				
Extraction fan				
Heater				
Toilet attached				
Number of power points				

NOTES

Checklist	Good	Average	Poor	Additional Notes
Outdoor Steps and sidewalk				
Outdoor Paint				
Driveway				
Outdoor Plantation				
Outdoor Entry Way				
Indoor Entry Way				
Doors				
Doors Fixtures				
Flooring				
Carpeting				
Windows				
Window Screens				
Window Fixtures				
Window Furnishings				
Ceilings				
Light Fixtures				
Staircases				
Indoor Paint				
Electrical Outlets and Fixtures				
Shelving				
Bedrooms				
Wardrobes and Closets				
Living Room (s)				
Dining Room (s)				
Dens (s)				
Study (s)				
Storage				
Fireplaces				
Bathroom Tiles				
Bathroom Faucets				

Notes:

_____

_____

_____

_____

Address _____   Price _____

Bedrooms _____   Bathrooms _____   Sq.Ft. _____

Lot Size: _____   Year Built _____   School District _____

Annual Tax _____

EXTERIOR

	Good	Average	Poor
View/Yard/Landscaping	☐	☐	☐
Trees	☐	☐	☐
Lawn (Front)	☐	☐	☐
Lawn (Back)	☐	☐	☐
Fences (condition)	☐	☐	☐
Landscaping (condition)	☐	☐	☐
Irrigation / Sprinkler	☐	☐	☐
	☐	☐	☐
House Type	☐	☐	☐
Exterior Siding	☐	☐	☐
Deck / Patio / Porch	☐	☐	☐
Garage	☐	☐	☐
Window / Doors	☐	☐	☐
Roof / Gutters	☐	☐	☐
Fencing	☐	☐	☐

HOME SYSTEMS

	Good	Average	Poor
Electrical	☐	☐	☐
Air Conditioning / Fans	☐	☐	☐
Heating	☐	☐	☐
Security	☐	☐	☐
Plumbing	☐	☐	☐
Intercom	☐	☐	☐

FEATURES

	Good	Average	Poor
Home Warranty	☐	☐	☐
Energy Saving Features	☐	☐	☐

INTERIOR

	Good	Average	Poor
Walls / Trim / Ceilings	☐	☐	☐
Flooring	☐	☐	☐
Stairs	☐	☐	☐
Storage	☐	☐	☐
Living Room	☐	☐	☐
Family Room	☐	☐	☐
Dining Room	☐	☐	☐

	Good	Average	Poor
Master Bedroom	☐	☐	☐
Bedroom 2	☐	☐	☐
Bedroom 3	☐	☐	☐
Bedroom 4	☐	☐	☐
Master Bathroom	☐	☐	☐
Bathroom 2	☐	☐	☐
Bathroom 3	☐	☐	☐
Bonus / Game Room	☐	☐	☐

	Good	Average	Poor
Kitchen	☐	☐	☐
Cabinets	☐	☐	☐
Countertop	☐	☐	☐
Counter Space	☐	☐	☐
Flooring	☐	☐	☐
Oven / Stove	☐	☐	☐
Microwave	☐	☐	☐
Layout	☐	☐	☐
Light Fixtures	☐	☐	☐
Backsplash	☐	☐	☐
Pantry	☐	☐	☐
Appliances	☐	☐	☐
Island	☐	☐	☐

	Good	Average	Poor
Basement	☐	☐	☐
Garage	☐	☐	☐

COMMUNITY

	Good	Average	Poor
Immediate Neighborhood	☐	☐	☐
Close to Employment	☐	☐	☐
Close to Shopping	☐	☐	☐
Close to Transportation	☐	☐	☐
Close to Schools / Daycare	☐	☐	☐
Close to Places of Worship	☐	☐	☐
Near Recreational Facilities	☐	☐	☐
Close to Airport	☐	☐	☐
Near Police and Fire Department	☐	☐	☐

Property Inspection Checklist

PROPERTY DETAILS

BEDROOMS		1	2	3	4	BATHROOMS		1	2	3
Flooring	Carpet					Flooring	Tiles			
	Floorboards						Other			
	Tiles						Cracks			
	Stained					Walls	Tiles			
	Scratched						Paint			
	Cracks						Wallpaper			
Walls	Paint						Cracks			
	Wallpaper						Damp patches			
	Cracks					Windows	Flyscreens			
	Damp patches						Blinds			
Windows	Flyscreens						Curtains			
	Blinds						Lockable			
	Curtains					Water pressure	High			
	Lockable						Medium			
Balcony							Low			
Ensuite						Shower	Free standing			
Built-in wardrobe							Over bath			
Air conditioning						Bath				
Ceiling fan						Vanity				
Gas outlet						Cupboards				
TV aerial outlet						Towel rails				
Phone line						Extraction fan				
Smoke alarm						Heater				
Number of power points						Toilet attached				
Dimensions (metres)		x	x	x	x	Number of power points				

NOTES

Checklist	Good	Average	Poor	Additional Notes
Outdoor Steps and sidewalk				
Outdoor Paint				
Driveway				
Outdoor Plantation				
Outdoor Entry Way				
Indoor Entry Way				
Doors				
Doors Fixtures				
Flooring				
Carpeting				
Windows				
Window Screens				
Window Fixtures				
Window Furnishings				
Ceilings				
Light Fixtures				
Staircases				
Indoor Paint				
Electrical Outlets and Fixtures				
Shelving				
Bedrooms				
Wardrobes and Closets				
Living Room (s)				
Dining Room (s)				
Dens (s)				
Study (s)				
Storage				
Fireplaces				
Bathroom Tiles				
Bathroom Faucets				

Notes:

_____

_____

_____

_____

Address _____ Price _____

Bedrooms _____ Bathrooms _____ Sq.Ft. _____

Lot Size: _____ Year Built _____ School District _____

Annual Tax _____

EXTERIOR

	Good	Average	Poor
View/Yard/Landscaping	☐	☐	☐
Trees	☐	☐	☐
Lawn (Front)	☐	☐	☐
Lawn (Back)	☐	☐	☐
Fences (condition)	☐	☐	☐
Landscaping (condition)	☐	☐	☐
Irrigation / Sprinkler	☐	☐	☐
	☐	☐	☐
House Type	☐	☐	☐
Exterior Siding	☐	☐	☐
Deck / Patio / Porch	☐	☐	☐
Garage	☐	☐	☐
Window / Doors	☐	☐	☐
Roof / Gutters	☐	☐	☐
Fencing	☐	☐	☐

HOME SYSTEMS

	Good	Average	Poor
Electrical	☐	☐	☐
Air Conditioning / Fans	☐	☐	☐
Heating	☐	☐	☐
Security	☐	☐	☐
Plumbing	☐	☐	☐
Intercom	☐	☐	☐

FEATURES

	Good	Average	Poor
Home Warranty	☐	☐	☐
Energy Saving Features	☐	☐	☐

INTERIOR

	Good	Average	Poor
Walls / Trim / Ceilings	☐	☐	☐
Flooring	☐	☐	☐
Stairs	☐	☐	☐
Storage	☐	☐	☐
Living Room	☐	☐	☐
Family Room	☐	☐	☐
Dining Room	☐	☐	☐

	Good	Average	Poor
Master Bedroom	☐	☐	☐
Bedroom 2	☐	☐	☐
Bedroom 3	☐	☐	☐
Bedroom 4	☐	☐	☐
Master Bathroom	☐	☐	☐
Bathroom 2	☐	☐	☐
Bathroom 3	☐	☐	☐
Bonus / Game Room	☐	☐	☐

	Good	Average	Poor
Kitchen	☐	☐	☐
Cabinets	☐	☐	☐
Countertop	☐	☐	☐
Counter Space	☐	☐	☐
Flooring	☐	☐	☐
Oven / Stove	☐	☐	☐
Microwave	☐	☐	☐
Layout	☐	☐	☐
Light Fixtures	☐	☐	☐
Backsplash	☐	☐	☐
Pantry	☐	☐	☐
Appliances	☐	☐	☐
Island	☐	☐	☐

	Good	Average	Poor
Basement	☐	☐	☐
Garage	☐	☐	☐

COMMUNITY

	Good	Average	Poor
Immediate Neighborhood	☐	☐	☐
Close to Employment	☐	☐	☐
Close to Shopping	☐	☐	☐
Close to Transportation	☐	☐	☐
Close to Schools / Daycare	☐	☐	☐
Close to Places of Worship	☐	☐	☐
Near Recreational Facilities	☐	☐	☐
Close to Airport	☐	☐	☐
Near Police and Fire Department	☐	☐	☐

Property Inspection Checklist

PROPERTY DETAILS

BEDROOMS		1	2	3	4
Flooring	Carpet				
	Floorboards				
	Tiles				
	Stained				
	Scratched				
	Cracks				
Walls	Paint				
	Wallpaper				
	Cracks				
	Damp patches				
Windows	Flyscreens				
	Blinds				
	Curtains				
	Lockable				
Balcony					
Ensuite					
Built-in wardrobe					
Air conditioning					
Ceiling fan					
Gas outlet					
TV aerial outlet					
Phone line					
Smoke alarm					
Number of power points					
Dimensions (metres)		x	x	x	x

BATHROOMS		1	2	3
Flooring	Tiles			
	Other			
	Cracks			
Walls	Tiles			
	Paint			
	Wallpaper			
	Cracks			
	Damp patches			
Windows	Flyscreens			
	Blinds			
	Curtains			
	Lockable			
Water pressure	High			
	Medium			
	Low			
Shower	Free standing			
	Over bath			
Bath				
Vanity				
Cupboards				
Towel rails				
Extraction fan				
Heater				
Toilet attached				
Number of power points				

NOTES

Checklist	Good	Average	Poor	Additional Notes
Outdoor Steps and sidewalk				
Outdoor Paint				
Driveway				
Outdoor Plantation				
Outdoor Entry Way				
Indoor Entry Way				
Doors				
Doors Fixtures				
Flooring				
Carpeting				
Windows				
Window Screens				
Window Fixtures				
Window Furnishings				
Ceilings				
Light Fixtures				
Staircases				
Indoor Paint				
Electrical Outlets and Fixtures				
Shelving				
Bedrooms				
Wardrobes and Closets				
Living Room (s)				
Dining Room (s)				
Dens (s)				
Study (s)				
Storage				
Fireplaces				
Bathroom Tiles				
Bathroom Faucets				

Notes:
_____
_____
_____
_____

Address _____ Price _____

Bedrooms _____ Bathrooms _____ Sq.Ft. _____

Lot Size: _____ Year Built _____ School District _____

Annual Tax _____

EXTERIOR

	Good	Average	Poor
View/Yard/Landscaping	☐	☐	☐
Trees	☐	☐	☐
Lawn (Front)	☐	☐	☐
Lawn (Back)	☐	☐	☐
Fences (condition)	☐	☐	☐
Landscaping (condition)	☐	☐	☐
Irrigation / Sprinkler	☐	☐	☐
	☐	☐	☐
House Type	☐	☐	☐
Exterior Siding	☐	☐	☐
Deck / Patio / Porch	☐	☐	☐
Garage	☐	☐	☐
Window / Doors	☐	☐	☐
Roof / Gutters	☐	☐	☐
Fencing	☐	☐	☐

HOME SYSTEMS

	Good	Average	Poor
Electrical	☐	☐	☐
Air Conditioning / Fans	☐	☐	☐
Heating	☐	☐	☐
Security	☐	☐	☐
Plumbing	☐	☐	☐
Intercom	☐	☐	☐

FEATURES

	Good	Average	Poor
Home Warranty	☐	☐	☐
Energy Saving Features	☐	☐	☐

INTERIOR

	Good	Average	Poor
Walls / Trim / Ceilings	☐	☐	☐
Flooring	☐	☐	☐
Stairs	☐	☐	☐
Storage	☐	☐	☐
Living Room	☐	☐	☐
Family Room	☐	☐	☐
Dining Room	☐	☐	☐

	Good	Average	Poor
Master Bedroom	☐	☐	☐
Bedroom 2	☐	☐	☐
Bedroom 3	☐	☐	☐
Bedroom 4	☐	☐	☐
Master Bathroom	☐	☐	☐
Bathroom 2	☐	☐	☐
Bathroom 3	☐	☐	☐
Bonus / Game Room	☐	☐	☐

	Good	Average	Poor
Kitchen			
Cabinets	☐	☐	☐
Countertop	☐	☐	☐
Counter Space	☐	☐	☐
Flooring	☐	☐	☐
Oven / Stove	☐	☐	☐
Microwave	☐	☐	☐
Layout	☐	☐	☐
Light Fixtures	☐	☐	☐
Backsplash	☐	☐	☐
Pantry	☐	☐	☐
Appliances	☐	☐	☐
Island	☐	☐	☐

	Good	Average	Poor
Basement	☐	☐	☐
Garage	☐	☐	☐

COMMUNITY

	Good	Average	Poor
Immediate Neighborhood	☐	☐	☐
Close to Employment	☐	☐	☐
Close to Shopping	☐	☐	☐
Close to Transportation	☐	☐	☐
Close to Schools / Daycare	☐	☐	☐
Close to Places of Worship	☐	☐	☐
Near Recreational Facilities	☐	☐	☐
Close to Airport	☐	☐	☐
Near Police and Fire Department	☐	☐	☐

Property Inspection Checklist

PROPERTY DETAILS

BEDROOMS		1	2	3	4
Flooring	Carpet				
	Floorboards				
	Tiles				
	Stained				
	Scratched				
	Cracks				
Walls	Paint				
	Wallpaper				
	Cracks				
	Damp patches				
Windows	Flyscreens				
	Blinds				
	Curtains				
	Lockable				
Balcony					
Ensuite					
Built-in wardrobe					
Air conditioning					
Ceiling fan					
Gas outlet					
TV aerial outlet					
Phone line					
Smoke alarm					
Number of power points					
Dimensions (metres)		X	X	X	X

BATHROOMS		1	2	3
Flooring	Tiles			
	Other			
	Cracks			
Walls	Tiles			
	Paint			
	Wallpaper			
	Cracks			
	Damp patches			
Windows	Flyscreens			
	Blinds			
	Curtains			
	Lockable			
Water pressure	High			
	Medium			
	Low			
Shower	Free standing			
	Over bath			
Bath				
Vanity				
Cupboards				
Towel rails				
Extraction fan				
Heater				
Toilet attached				
Number of power points				

NOTES

Checklist	Good	Average	Poor	Additional Notes
Outdoor Steps and sidewalk				
Outdoor Paint				
Driveway				
Outdoor Plantation				
Outdoor Entry Way				
Indoor Entry Way				
Doors				
Doors Fixtures				
Flooring				
Carpeting				
Windows				
Window Screens				
Window Fixtures				
Window Furnishings				
Ceilings				
Light Fixtures				
Staircases				
Indoor Paint				
Electrical Outlets and Fixtures				
Shelving				
Bedrooms				
Wardrobes and Closets				
Living Room (s)				
Dining Room (s)				
Dens (s)				
Study (s)				
Storage				
Fireplaces				
Bathroom Tiles				
Bathroom Faucets				

Notes:

_____

_____

_____

_____

Address _____ Price _____

Bedrooms _____ Bathrooms _____ Sq.Ft. _____

Lot Size: _____ Year Built _____ School District _____

Annual Tax _____

EXTERIOR

	Good	Average	Poor
View/Yard/Landscaping	☐	☐	☐
Trees	☐	☐	☐
Lawn (Front)	☐	☐	☐
Lawn (Back)	☐	☐	☐
Fences (condition)	☐	☐	☐
Landscaping (condition)	☐	☐	☐
Irrigation / Sprinkler	☐	☐	☐
	☐	☐	☐
House Type	☐	☐	☐
Exterior Siding	☐	☐	☐
Deck / Patio / Porch	☐	☐	☐
Garage	☐	☐	☐
Window / Doors	☐	☐	☐
Roof / Gutters	☐	☐	☐
Fencing	☐	☐	☐

HOME SYSTEMS

	Good	Average	Poor
Electrical	☐	☐	☐
Air Conditioning / Fans	☐	☐	☐
Heating	☐	☐	☐
Security	☐	☐	☐
Plumbing	☐	☐	☐
Intercom	☐	☐	☐

FEATURES

	Good	Average	Poor
Home Warranty	☐	☐	☐
Energy Saving Features	☐	☐	☐

INTERIOR

	Good	Average	Poor
Walls / Trim / Ceilings	☐	☐	☐
Flooring	☐	☐	☐
Stairs	☐	☐	☐
Storage	☐	☐	☐
Living Room	☐	☐	☐
Family Room	☐	☐	☐
Dining Room	☐	☐	☐

	Good	Average	Poor
Master Bedroom	☐	☐	☐
Bedroom 2	☐	☐	☐
Bedroom 3	☐	☐	☐
Bedroom 4	☐	☐	☐
Master Bathroom	☐	☐	☐
Bathroom 2	☐	☐	☐
Bathroom 3	☐	☐	☐
Bonus / Game Room	☐	☐	☐

	Good	Average	Poor
Kitchen	☐	☐	☐
Cabinets	☐	☐	☐
Countertop	☐	☐	☐
Counter Space	☐	☐	☐
Flooring	☐	☐	☐
Oven / Stove	☐	☐	☐
Microwave	☐	☐	☐
Layout	☐	☐	☐
Light Fixtures	☐	☐	☐
Backsplash	☐	☐	☐
Pantry	☐	☐	☐
Appliances	☐	☐	☐
Island	☐	☐	☐

	Good	Average	Poor
Basement	☐	☐	☐
Garage	☐	☐	☐

COMMUNITY

	Good	Average	Poor
Immediate Neighborhood	☐	☐	☐
Close to Employment	☐	☐	☐
Close to Shopping	☐	☐	☐
Close to Transportation	☐	☐	☐
Close to Schools / Daycare	☐	☐	☐
Close to Places of Worship	☐	☐	☐
Near Recreational Facilities	☐	☐	☐
Close to Airport	☐	☐	☐
Near Police and Fire Department	☐	☐	☐

Property Inspection Checklist

PROPERTY DETAILS

BEDROOMS		1	2	3	4
Flooring	Carpet				
	Floorboards				
	Tiles				
	Stained				
	Scratched				
	Cracks				
Walls	Paint				
	Wallpaper				
	Cracks				
	Damp patches				
Windows	Flyscreens				
	Blinds				
	Curtains				
	Lockable				
Balcony					
Ensuite					
Built-in wardrobe					
Air conditioning					
Ceiling fan					
Gas outlet					
TV aerial outlet					
Phone line					
Smoke alarm					
Number of power points					
Dimensions (metres)		x	x	x	x

BATHROOMS		1	2	3
Flooring	Tiles			
	Other			
	Cracks			
Walls	Tiles			
	Paint			
	Wallpaper			
	Cracks			
	Damp patches			
Windows	Flyscreens			
	Blinds			
	Curtains			
	Lockable			
Water pressure	High			
	Medium			
	Low			
Shower	Free standing			
	Over bath			
Bath				
Vanity				
Cupboards				
Towel rails				
Extraction fan				
Heater				
Toilet attached				
Number of power points				

NOTES

Checklist	Good	Average	Poor	Additional Notes
Outdoor Steps and sidewalk				
Outdoor Paint				
Driveway				
Outdoor Plantation				
Outdoor Entry Way				
Indoor Entry Way				
Doors				
Doors Fixtures				
Flooring				
Carpeting				
Windows				
Window Screens				
Window Fixtures				
Window Furnishings				
Ceilings				
Light Fixtures				
Staircases				
Indoor Paint				
Electrical Outlets and Fixtures				
Shelving				
Bedrooms				
Wardrobes and Closets				
Living Room (s)				
Dining Room (s)				
Dens (s)				
Study (s)				
Storage				
Fireplaces				
Bathroom Tiles				
Bathroom Faucets				

Notes:
_____
_____
_____
_____

Address _____   Price _____

Bedrooms _____   Bathrooms _____   Sq.Ft. _____

Lot Size: _____   Year Built _____   School District _____

Annual Tax _____

EXTERIOR

	Good	Average	Poor
View/Yard/Landscaping	☐	☐	☐
Trees	☐	☐	☐
Lawn (Front)	☐	☐	☐
Lawn (Back)	☐	☐	☐
Fences (condition)	☐	☐	☐
Landscaping (condition)	☐	☐	☐
Irrigation / Sprinkler	☐	☐	☐
House Type	☐	☐	☐
Exterior Siding	☐	☐	☐
Deck / Patio / Porch	☐	☐	☐
Garage	☐	☐	☐
Window / Doors	☐	☐	☐
Roof / Gutters	☐	☐	☐
Fencing	☐	☐	☐

HOME SYSTEMS

	Good	Average	Poor
Electrical	☐	☐	☐
Air Conditioning / Fans	☐	☐	☐
Heating	☐	☐	☐
Security	☐	☐	☐
Plumbing	☐	☐	☐
Intercom	☐	☐	☐

FEATURES

	Good	Average	Poor
Home Warranty	☐	☐	☐
Energy Saving Features	☐	☐	☐

INTERIOR

	Good	Average	Poor
Walls / Trim / Ceilings	☐	☐	☐
Flooring	☐	☐	☐
Stairs	☐	☐	☐
Storage	☐	☐	☐
Living Room	☐	☐	☐
Family Room	☐	☐	☐
Dining Room	☐	☐	☐

	Good	Average	Poor
Master Bedroom	☐	☐	☐
Bedroom 2	☐	☐	☐
Bedroom 3	☐	☐	☐
Bedroom 4	☐	☐	☐
Master Bathroom	☐	☐	☐
Bathroom 2	☐	☐	☐
Bathroom 3	☐	☐	☐
Bonus / Game Room	☐	☐	☐

	Good	Average	Poor
Kitchen	☐	☐	☐
Cabinets	☐	☐	☐
Countertop	☐	☐	☐
Counter Space	☐	☐	☐
Flooring	☐	☐	☐
Oven / Stove	☐	☐	☐
Microwave	☐	☐	☐
Layout	☐	☐	☐
Light Fixtures	☐	☐	☐
Backsplash	☐	☐	☐
Pantry	☐	☐	☐
Appliances	☐	☐	☐
Island	☐	☐	☐

	Good	Average	Poor
Basement	☐	☐	☐
Garage	☐	☐	☐

COMMUNITY

	Good	Average	Poor
Immediate Neighborhood	☐	☐	☐
Close to Employment	☐	☐	☐
Close to Shopping	☐	☐	☐
Close to Transportation	☐	☐	☐
Close to Schools / Daycare	☐	☐	☐
Close to Places of Worship	☐	☐	☐
Near Recreational Facilities	☐	☐	☐
Close to Airport	☐	☐	☐
Near Police and Fire Department	☐	☐	☐

Property Inspection Checklist

PROPERTY DETAILS

BEDROOMS		1	2	3	4
Flooring	Carpet				
	Floorboards				
	Tiles				
	Stained				
	Scratched				
	Cracks				
Walls	Paint				
	Wallpaper				
	Cracks				
	Damp patches				
Windows	Flyscreens				
	Blinds				
	Curtains				
	Lockable				
Balcony					
Ensuite					
Built-in wardrobe					
Air conditioning					
Ceiling fan					
Gas outlet					
TV aerial outlet					
Phone line					
Smoke alarm					
Number of power points					
Dimensions (metres)		x	x	x	x

BATHROOMS		1	2	3
Flooring	Tiles			
	Other			
	Cracks			
Walls	Tiles			
	Paint			
	Wallpaper			
	Cracks			
	Damp patches			
Windows	Flyscreens			
	Blinds			
	Curtains			
	Lockable			
Water pressure	High			
	Medium			
	Low			
Shower	Free standing			
	Over bath			
Bath				
Vanity				
Cupboards				
Towel rails				
Extraction fan				
Heater				
Toilet attached				
Number of power points				

NOTES

Checklist	Good	Average	Poor	Additional Notes
Outdoor Steps and sidewalk				
Outdoor Paint				
Driveway				
Outdoor Plantation				
Outdoor Entry Way				
Indoor Entry Way				
Doors				
Doors Fixtures				
Flooring				
Carpeting				
Windows				
Window Screens				
Window Fixtures				
Window Furnishings				
Ceilings				
Light Fixtures				
Staircases				
Indoor Paint				
Electrical Outlets and Fixtures				
Shelving				
Bedrooms				
Wardrobes and Closets				
Living Room (s)				
Dining Room (s)				
Dens (s)				
Study (s)				
Storage				
Fireplaces				
Bathroom Tiles				
Bathroom Faucets				

Notes:

_____

_____

_____

_____

Address _____ Price _____

Bedrooms _____ Bathrooms _____ Sq.Ft. _____

Lot Size: _____ Year Built _____ School District _____

Annual Tax _____

EXTERIOR

	Good	Average	Poor
View/Yard/Landscaping	☐	☐	☐
Trees	☐	☐	☐
Lawn (Front)	☐	☐	☐
Lawn (Back)	☐	☐	☐
Fences (condition)	☐	☐	☐
Landscaping (condition)	☐	☐	☐
Irrigation / Sprinkler	☐	☐	☐
	☐	☐	☐
House Type	☐	☐	☐
Exterior Siding	☐	☐	☐
Deck / Patio / Porch	☐	☐	☐
Garage	☐	☐	☐
Window / Doors	☐	☐	☐
Roof / Gutters	☐	☐	☐
Fencing	☐	☐	☐

HOME SYSTEMS

	Good	Average	Poor
Electrical	☐	☐	☐
Air Conditioning / Fans	☐	☐	☐
Heating	☐	☐	☐
Security	☐	☐	☐
Plumbing	☐	☐	☐
Intercom	☐	☐	☐

FEATURES

	Good	Average	Poor
Home Warranty	☐	☐	☐
Energy Saving Features	☐	☐	☐

INTERIOR

	Good	Average	Poor
Walls / Trim / Ceilings	☐	☐	☐
Flooring	☐	☐	☐
Stairs	☐	☐	☐
Storage	☐	☐	☐
Living Room	☐	☐	☐
Family Room	☐	☐	☐
Dining Room	☐	☐	☐

	Good	Average	Poor
Master Bedroom	☐	☐	☐
Bedroom 2	☐	☐	☐
Bedroom 3	☐	☐	☐
Bedroom 4	☐	☐	☐
Master Bathroom	☐	☐	☐
Bathroom 2	☐	☐	☐
Bathroom 3	☐	☐	☐
Bonus / Game Room	☐	☐	☐

	Good	Average	Poor
Kitchen	☐	☐	☐
Cabinets	☐	☐	☐
Countertop	☐	☐	☐
Counter Space	☐	☐	☐
Flooring	☐	☐	☐
Oven / Stove	☐	☐	☐
Microwave	☐	☐	☐
Layout	☐	☐	☐
Light Fixtures	☐	☐	☐
Backsplash	☐	☐	☐
Pantry	☐	☐	☐
Appliances	☐	☐	☐
Island	☐	☐	☐

	Good	Average	Poor
Basement	☐	☐	☐
Garage	☐	☐	☐

COMMUNITY

	Good	Average	Poor
Immediate Neighborhood	☐	☐	☐
Close to Employment	☐	☐	☐
Close to Shopping	☐	☐	☐
Close to Transportation	☐	☐	☐
Close to Schools / Daycare	☐	☐	☐
Close to Places of Worship	☐	☐	☐
Near Recreational Facilities	☐	☐	☐
Close to Airport	☐	☐	☐
Near Police and Fire Department	☐	☐	☐

Property Inspection Checklist

PROPERTY DETAILS

BEDROOMS		1	2	3	4
Flooring	Carpet				
	Floorboards				
	Tiles				
	Stained				
	Scratched				
	Cracks				
Walls	Paint				
	Wallpaper				
	Cracks				
	Damp patches				
Windows	Flyscreens				
	Blinds				
	Curtains				
	Lockable				
Balcony					
Ensuite					
Built-in wardrobe					
Air conditioning					
Ceiling fan					
Gas outlet					
TV aerial outlet					
Phone line					
Smoke alarm					
Number of power points					
Dimensions (metres)		x	x	x	x

BATHROOMS		1	2	3
Flooring	Tiles			
	Other			
	Cracks			
Walls	Tiles			
	Paint			
	Wallpaper			
	Cracks			
	Damp patches			
Windows	Flyscreens			
	Blinds			
	Curtains			
	Lockable			
Water pressure	High			
	Medium			
	Low			
Shower	Free standing			
	Over bath			
Bath				
Vanity				
Cupboards				
Towel rails				
Extraction fan				
Heater				
Toilet attached				
Number of power points				

NOTES

Checklist	Good	Average	Poor	Additional Notes
Outdoor Steps and sidewalk				
Outdoor Paint				
Driveway				
Outdoor Plantation				
Outdoor Entry Way				
Indoor Entry Way				
Doors				
Doors Fixtures				
Flooring				
Carpeting				
Windows				
Window Screens				
Window Fixtures				
Window Furnishings				
Ceilings				
Light Fixtures				
Staircases				
Indoor Paint				
Electrical Outlets and Fixtures				
Shelving				
Bedrooms				
Wardrobes and Closets				
Living Room (s)				
Dining Room (s)				
Dens (s)				
Study (s)				
Storage				
Fireplaces				
Bathroom Tiles				
Bathroom Faucets				

Notes:

_____

_____

_____

_____

Address _____ Price _____

Bedrooms _____ Bathrooms _____ Sq.Ft. _____

Lot Size: _____ Year Built _____ School District _____

Annual Tax _____

EXTERIOR

	Good	Average	Poor
View/Yard/Landscaping	☐	☐	☐
Trees	☐	☐	☐
Lawn (Front)	☐	☐	☐
Lawn (Back)	☐	☐	☐
Fences (condition)	☐	☐	☐
Landscaping (condition)	☐	☐	☐
Irrigation / Sprinkler	☐	☐	☐
	☐	☐	☐
House Type	☐	☐	☐
Exterior Siding	☐	☐	☐
Deck / Patio / Porch	☐	☐	☐
Garage	☐	☐	☐
Window / Doors	☐	☐	☐
Roof / Gutters	☐	☐	☐
Fencing	☐	☐	☐

HOME SYSTEMS

	Good	Average	Poor
Electrical	☐	☐	☐
Air Conditioning / Fans	☐	☐	☐
Heating	☐	☐	☐
Security	☐	☐	☐
Plumbing	☐	☐	☐
Intercom	☐	☐	☐

FEATURES

	Good	Average	Poor
Home Warranty	☐	☐	☐
Energy Saving Features	☐	☐	☐

INTERIOR

	Good	Average	Poor
Walls / Trim / Ceilings	☐	☐	☐
Flooring	☐	☐	☐
Stairs	☐	☐	☐
Storage	☐	☐	☐
Living Room	☐	☐	☐
Family Room	☐	☐	☐
Dining Room	☐	☐	☐

	Good	Average	Poor
Master Bedroom	☐	☐	☐
Bedroom 2	☐	☐	☐
Bedroom 3	☐	☐	☐
Bedroom 4	☐	☐	☐
Master Bathroom	☐	☐	☐
Bathroom 2	☐	☐	☐
Bathroom 3	☐	☐	☐
Bonus / Game Room	☐	☐	☐

	Good	Average	Poor
Kitchen			
Cabinets	☐	☐	☐
Countertop	☐	☐	☐
Counter Space	☐	☐	☐
Flooring	☐	☐	☐
Oven / Stove	☐	☐	☐
Microwave	☐	☐	☐
Layout	☐	☐	☐
Light Fixtures	☐	☐	☐
Backsplash	☐	☐	☐
Pantry	☐	☐	☐
Appliances	☐	☐	☐
Island	☐	☐	☐

	Good	Average	Poor
Basement	☐	☐	☐
Garage	☐	☐	☐

COMMUNITY

	Good	Average	Poor
Immediate Neighborhood	☐	☐	☐
Close to Employment	☐	☐	☐
Close to Shopping	☐	☐	☐
Close to Transportation	☐	☐	☐
Close to Schools / Daycare	☐	☐	☐
Close to Places of Worship	☐	☐	☐
Near Recreational Facilities	☐	☐	☐
Close to Airport	☐	☐	☐
Near Police and Fire Department	☐	☐	☐

Property Inspection Checklist

PROPERTY DETAILS

BEDROOMS

		1	2	3	4
Flooring	Carpet				
	Floorboards				
	Tiles				
	Stained				
	Scratched				
	Cracks				
Walls	Paint				
	Wallpaper				
	Cracks				
	Damp patches				
Windows	Flyscreens				
	Blinds				
	Curtains				
	Lockable				
Balcony					
Ensuite					
Built-in wardrobe					
Air conditioning					
Ceiling fan					
Gas outlet					
TV aerial outlet					
Phone line					
Smoke alarm					
Number of power points					
Dimensions (metres)		X	X	X	X

BATHROOMS

		1	2	3
Flooring	Tiles			
	Other			
	Cracks			
Walls	Tiles			
	Paint			
	Wallpaper			
	Cracks			
	Damp patches			
Windows	Flyscreens			
	Blinds			
	Curtains			
	Lockable			
Water pressure	High			
	Medium			
	Low			
Shower	Free standing			
	Over bath			
Bath				
Vanity				
Cupboards				
Towel rails				
Extraction fan				
Heater				
Toilet attached				
Number of power points				

NOTES

Checklist	Good	Average	Poor	Additional Notes
Outdoor Steps and sidewalk				
Outdoor Paint				
Driveway				
Outdoor Plantation				
Outdoor Entry Way				
Indoor Entry Way				
Doors				
Doors Fixtures				
Flooring				
Carpeting				
Windows				
Window Screens				
Window Fixtures				
Window Furnishings				
Ceilings				
Light Fixtures				
Staircases				
Indoor Paint				
Electrical Outlets and Fixtures				
Shelving				
Bedrooms				
Wardrobes and Closets				
Living Room (s)				
Dining Room (s)				
Dens (s)				
Study (s)				
Storage				
Fireplaces				
Bathroom Tiles				
Bathroom Faucets				

Notes:
_____
_____
_____
_____

Address _____ Price _____

Bedrooms _____ Bathrooms _____ Sq.Ft. _____

Lot Size: _____ Year Built _____ School District _____

Annual Tax _____

EXTERIOR

	Good	Average	Poor
View/Yard/Landscaping	☐	☐	☐
Trees	☐	☐	☐
Lawn (Front)	☐	☐	☐
Lawn (Back)	☐	☐	☐
Fences (condition)	☐	☐	☐
Landscaping (condition)	☐	☐	☐
Irrigation / Sprinkler	☐	☐	☐
	☐	☐	☐
House Type	☐	☐	☐
Exterior Siding	☐	☐	☐
Deck / Patio / Porch	☐	☐	☐
Garage	☐	☐	☐
Window / Doors	☐	☐	☐
Roof / Gutters	☐	☐	☐
Fencing	☐	☐	☐

HOME SYSTEMS

	Good	Average	Poor
Electrical	☐	☐	☐
Air Conditioning / Fans	☐	☐	☐
Heating	☐	☐	☐
Security	☐	☐	☐
Plumbing	☐	☐	☐
Intercom	☐	☐	☐

FEATURES

	Good	Average	Poor
Home Warranty	☐	☐	☐
Energy Saving Features	☐	☐	☐

INTERIOR

	Good	Average	Poor
Walls / Trim / Ceilings	☐	☐	☐
Flooring	☐	☐	☐
Stairs	☐	☐	☐
Storage	☐	☐	☐
Living Room	☐	☐	☐
Family Room	☐	☐	☐
Dining Room	☐	☐	☐

	Good	Average	Poor
Master Bedroom	☐	☐	☐
Bedroom 2	☐	☐	☐
Bedroom 3	☐	☐	☐
Bedroom 4	☐	☐	☐
Master Bathroom	☐	☐	☐
Bathroom 2	☐	☐	☐
Bathroom 3	☐	☐	☐
Bonus / Game Room	☐	☐	☐

	Good	Average	Poor
Kitchen	☐	☐	☐
Cabinets	☐	☐	☐
Countertop	☐	☐	☐
Counter Space	☐	☐	☐
Flooring	☐	☐	☐
Oven / Stove	☐	☐	☐
Microwave	☐	☐	☐
Layout	☐	☐	☐
Light Fixtures	☐	☐	☐
Backsplash	☐	☐	☐
Pantry	☐	☐	☐
Appliances	☐	☐	☐
Island	☐	☐	☐

	Good	Average	Poor
Basement	☐	☐	☐
Garage	☐	☐	☐

COMMUNITY

	Good	Average	Poor
Immediate Neighborhood	☐	☐	☐
Close to Employment	☐	☐	☐
Close to Shopping	☐	☐	☐
Close to Transportation	☐	☐	☐
Close to Schools / Daycare	☐	☐	☐
Close to Places of Worship	☐	☐	☐
Near Recreational Facilities	☐	☐	☐
Close to Airport	☐	☐	☐
Near Police and Fire Department	☐	☐	☐

Property Inspection Checklist

PROPERTY DETAILS

BEDROOMS		1	2	3	4
Flooring	Carpet				
	Floorboards				
	Tiles				
	Stained				
	Scratched				
	Cracks				
Walls	Paint				
	Wallpaper				
	Cracks				
	Damp patches				
Windows	Flyscreens				
	Blinds				
	Curtains				
	Lockable				
Balcony					
Ensuite					
Built-in wardrobe					
Air conditioning					
Ceiling fan					
Gas outlet					
TV aerial outlet					
Phone line					
Smoke alarm					
Number of power points					
Dimensions (metres)		x	x	x	x

BATHROOMS		1	2	3
Flooring	Tiles			
	Other			
	Cracks			
Walls	Tiles			
	Paint			
	Wallpaper			
	Cracks			
	Damp patches			
Windows	Flyscreens			
	Blinds			
	Curtains			
	Lockable			
Water pressure	High			
	Medium			
	Low			
Shower	Free standing			
	Over bath			
Bath				
Vanity				
Cupboards				
Towel rails				
Extraction fan				
Heater				
Toilet attached				
Number of power points				

NOTES

Checklist	Good	Average	Poor	Additional Notes
Outdoor Steps and sidewalk				
Outdoor Paint				
Driveway				
Outdoor Plantation				
Outdoor Entry Way				
Indoor Entry Way				
Doors				
Doors Fixtures				
Flooring				
Carpeting				
Windows				
Window Screens				
Window Fixtures				
Window Furnishings				
Ceilings				
Light Fixtures				
Staircases				
Indoor Paint				
Electrical Outlets and Fixtures				
Shelving				
Bedrooms				
Wardrobes and Closets				
Living Room (s)				
Dining Room (s)				
Dens (s)				
Study (s)				
Storage				
Fireplaces				
Bathroom Tiles				
Bathroom Faucets				

Notes:

_____

_____

_____

_____

_____

Address _____ Price _____

Bedrooms _____ Bathrooms _____ Sq.Ft. _____

Lot Size: _____ Year Built _____ School District _____

Annual Tax _____

EXTERIOR

	Good	Average	Poor
View/Yard/Landscaping	☐	☐	☐
Trees	☐	☐	☐
Lawn (Front)	☐	☐	☐
Lawn (Back)	☐	☐	☐
Fences (condition)	☐	☐	☐
Landscaping (condition)	☐	☐	☐
Irrigation / Sprinkler	☐	☐	☐
House Type	☐	☐	☐
Exterior Siding	☐	☐	☐
Deck / Patio / Porch	☐	☐	☐
Garage	☐	☐	☐
Window / Doors	☐	☐	☐
Roof / Gutters	☐	☐	☐
Fencing	☐	☐	☐

HOME SYSTEMS

	Good	Average	Poor
Electrical	☐	☐	☐
Air Conditioning / Fans	☐	☐	☐
Heating	☐	☐	☐
Security	☐	☐	☐
Plumbing	☐	☐	☐
Intercom	☐	☐	☐

FEATURES

	Good	Average	Poor
Home Warranty	☐	☐	☐
Energy Saving Features	☐	☐	☐

INTERIOR

	Good	Average	Poor
Walls / Trim / Ceilings	☐	☐	☐
Flooring	☐	☐	☐
Stairs	☐	☐	☐
Storage	☐	☐	☐
Living Room	☐	☐	☐
Family Room	☐	☐	☐
Dining Room	☐	☐	☐

	Good	Average	Poor
Master Bedroom	☐	☐	☐
Bedroom 2	☐	☐	☐
Bedroom 3	☐	☐	☐
Bedroom 4	☐	☐	☐
Master Bathroom	☐	☐	☐
Bathroom 2	☐	☐	☐
Bathroom 3	☐	☐	☐
Bonus / Game Room	☐	☐	☐

	Good	Average	Poor
Kitchen			
Cabinets	☐	☐	☐
Countertop	☐	☐	☐
Counter Space	☐	☐	☐
Flooring	☐	☐	☐
Oven / Stove	☐	☐	☐
Microwave	☐	☐	☐
Layout	☐	☐	☐
Light Fixtures	☐	☐	☐
Backsplash	☐	☐	☐
Pantry	☐	☐	☐
Appliances	☐	☐	☐
Island	☐	☐	☐

	Good	Average	Poor
Basement	☐	☐	☐
Garage	☐	☐	☐

COMMUNITY

	Good	Average	Poor
Immediate Neighborhood	☐	☐	☐
Close to Employment	☐	☐	☐
Close to Shopping	☐	☐	☐
Close to Transportation	☐	☐	☐
Close to Schools / Daycare	☐	☐	☐
Close to Places of Worship	☐	☐	☐
Near Recreational Facilities	☐	☐	☐
Close to Airport	☐	☐	☐
Near Police and Fire Department	☐	☐	☐

Property Inspection Checklist

PROPERTY DETAILS

BEDROOMS		1	2	3	4
Flooring	Carpet				
	Floorboards				
	Tiles				
	Stained				
	Scratched				
	Cracks				
Walls	Paint				
	Wallpaper				
	Cracks				
	Damp patches				
Windows	Flyscreens				
	Blinds				
	Curtains				
	Lockable				
Balcony					
Ensuite					
Built-in wardrobe					
Air conditioning					
Ceiling fan					
Gas outlet					
TV aerial outlet					
Phone line					
Smoke alarm					
Number of power points					
Dimensions (metres)		x	x	x	x

BATHROOMS		1	2	3
Flooring	Tiles			
	Other			
	Cracks			
Walls	Tiles			
	Paint			
	Wallpaper			
	Cracks			
	Damp patches			
Windows	Flyscreens			
	Blinds			
	Curtains			
	Lockable			
Water pressure	High			
	Medium			
	Low			
Shower	Free standing			
	Over bath			
Bath				
Vanity				
Cupboards				
Towel rails				
Extraction fan				
Heater				
Toilet attached				
Number of power points				

NOTES

Checklist	Good	Average	Poor	Additional Notes
Outdoor Steps and sidewalk				
Outdoor Paint				
Driveway				
Outdoor Plantation				
Outdoor Entry Way				
Indoor Entry Way				
Doors				
Doors Fixtures				
Flooring				
Carpeting				
Windows				
Window Screens				
Window Fixtures				
Window Furnishings				
Ceilings				
Light Fixtures				
Staircases				
Indoor Paint				
Electrical Outlets and Fixtures				
Shelving				
Bedrooms				
Wardrobes and Closets				
Living Room (s)				
Dining Room (s)				
Dens (s)				
Study (s)				
Storage				
Fireplaces				
Bathroom Tiles				
Bathroom Faucets				

Notes:

_____

_____

_____

_____

Address _____ Price _____

Bedrooms _____ Bathrooms _____ Sq.Ft. _____

Lot Size: _____ Year Built _____ School District _____

Annual Tax _____

EXTERIOR

	Good	Average	Poor
View/Yard/Landscaping	☐	☐	☐
Trees	☐	☐	☐
Lawn (Front)	☐	☐	☐
Lawn (Back)	☐	☐	☐
Fences (condition)	☐	☐	☐
Landscaping (condition)	☐	☐	☐
Irrigation / Sprinkler	☐	☐	☐
	☐	☐	☐
House Type	☐	☐	☐
Exterior Siding	☐	☐	☐
Deck / Patio / Porch	☐	☐	☐
Garage	☐	☐	☐
Window / Doors	☐	☐	☐
Roof / Gutters	☐	☐	☐
Fencing	☐	☐	☐

HOME SYSTEMS

	Good	Average	Poor
Electrical	☐	☐	☐
Air Conditioning / Fans	☐	☐	☐
Heating	☐	☐	☐
Security	☐	☐	☐
Plumbing	☐	☐	☐
Intercom	☐	☐	☐

FEATURES

	Good	Average	Poor
Home Warranty	☐	☐	☐
Energy Saving Features	☐	☐	☐

INTERIOR

	Good	Average	Poor
Walls / Trim / Ceilings	☐	☐	☐
Flooring	☐	☐	☐
Stairs	☐	☐	☐
Storage	☐	☐	☐
Living Room	☐	☐	☐
Family Room	☐	☐	☐
Dining Room	☐	☐	☐

	Good	Average	Poor
Master Bedroom	☐	☐	☐
Bedroom 2	☐	☐	☐
Bedroom 3	☐	☐	☐
Bedroom 4	☐	☐	☐
Master Bathroom	☐	☐	☐
Bathroom 2	☐	☐	☐
Bathroom 3	☐	☐	☐
Bonus / Game Room	☐	☐	☐

	Good	Average	Poor
Kitchen	☐	☐	☐
Cabinets	☐	☐	☐
Countertop	☐	☐	☐
Counter Space	☐	☐	☐
Flooring	☐	☐	☐
Oven / Stove	☐	☐	☐
Microwave	☐	☐	☐
Layout	☐	☐	☐
Light Fixtures	☐	☐	☐
Backsplash	☐	☐	☐
Pantry	☐	☐	☐
Appliances	☐	☐	☐
Island	☐	☐	☐

	Good	Average	Poor
Basement	☐	☐	☐
Garage	☐	☐	☐

COMMUNITY

	Good	Average	Poor
Immediate Neighborhood	☐	☐	☐
Close to Employment	☐	☐	☐
Close to Shopping	☐	☐	☐
Close to Transportation	☐	☐	☐
Close to Schools / Daycare	☐	☐	☐
Close to Places of Worship	☐	☐	☐
Near Recreational Facilities	☐	☐	☐
Close to Airport	☐	☐	☐
Near Police and Fire Department	☐	☐	☐

Property Inspection Checklist

PROPERTY DETAILS

BEDROOMS		1	2	3	4
Flooring	Carpet				
	Floorboards				
	Tiles				
	Stained				
	Scratched				
	Cracks				
Walls	Paint				
	Wallpaper				
	Cracks				
	Damp patches				
Windows	Flyscreens				
	Blinds				
	Curtains				
	Lockable				
Balcony					
Ensuite					
Built-in wardrobe					
Air conditioning					
Ceiling fan					
Gas outlet					
TV aerial outlet					
Phone line					
Smoke alarm					
Number of power points					
Dimensions (metres)		x	x	x	x

BATHROOMS		1	2	3
Flooring	Tiles			
	Other			
	Cracks			
Walls	Tiles			
	Paint			
	Wallpaper			
	Cracks			
	Damp patches			
Windows	Flyscreens			
	Blinds			
	Curtains			
	Lockable			
Water pressure	High			
	Medium			
	Low			
Shower	Free standing			
	Over bath			
Bath				
Vanity				
Cupboards				
Towel rails				
Extraction fan				
Heater				
Toilet attached				
Number of power points				

NOTES

Checklist	Good	Average	Poor	Additional Notes
Outdoor Steps and sidewalk				
Outdoor Paint				
Driveway				
Outdoor Plantation				
Outdoor Entry Way				
Indoor Entry Way				
Doors				
Doors Fixtures				
Flooring				
Carpeting				
Windows				
Window Screens				
Window Fixtures				
Window Furnishings				
Ceilings				
Light Fixtures				
Staircases				
Indoor Paint				
Electrical Outlets and Fixtures				
Shelving				
Bedrooms				
Wardrobes and Closets				
Living Room (s)				
Dining Room (s)				
Dens (s)				
Study (s)				
Storage				
Fireplaces				
Bathroom Tiles				
Bathroom Faucets				

Notes:

_____

_____

_____

_____

Address _____ Price _____

Bedrooms _____ Bathrooms _____ Sq.Ft. _____

Lot Size: _____ Year Built _____ School District _____

Annual Tax _____

EXTERIOR

	Good	Average	Poor
View/Yard/Landscaping	☐	☐	☐
Trees	☐	☐	☐
Lawn (Front)	☐	☐	☐
Lawn (Back)	☐	☐	☐
Fences (condition)	☐	☐	☐
Landscaping (condition)	☐	☐	☐
Irrigation / Sprinkler	☐	☐	☐
	☐	☐	☐
House Type	☐	☐	☐
Exterior Siding	☐	☐	☐
Deck / Patio / Porch	☐	☐	☐
Garage	☐	☐	☐
Window / Doors	☐	☐	☐
Roof / Gutters	☐	☐	☐
Fencing	☐	☐	☐

HOME SYSTEMS

	Good	Average	Poor
Electrical	☐	☐	☐
Air Conditioning / Fans	☐	☐	☐
Heating	☐	☐	☐
Security	☐	☐	☐
Plumbing	☐	☐	☐
Intercom	☐	☐	☐

FEATURES

	Good	Average	Poor
Home Warranty	☐	☐	☐
Energy Saving Features	☐	☐	☐

INTERIOR

	Good	Average	Poor
Walls / Trim / Ceilings	☐	☐	☐
Flooring	☐	☐	☐
Stairs	☐	☐	☐
Storage	☐	☐	☐
Living Room	☐	☐	☐
Family Room	☐	☐	☐
Dining Room	☐	☐	☐

	Good	Average	Poor
Master Bedroom	☐	☐	☐
Bedroom 2	☐	☐	☐
Bedroom 3	☐	☐	☐
Bedroom 4	☐	☐	☐
Master Bathroom	☐	☐	☐
Bathroom 2	☐	☐	☐
Bathroom 3	☐	☐	☐
Bonus / Game Room	☐	☐	☐

	Good	Average	Poor
Kitchen	☐	☐	☐
Cabinets	☐	☐	☐
Countertop	☐	☐	☐
Counter Space	☐	☐	☐
Flooring	☐	☐	☐
Oven / Stove	☐	☐	☐
Microwave	☐	☐	☐
Layout	☐	☐	☐
Light Fixtures	☐	☐	☐
Backsplash	☐	☐	☐
Pantry	☐	☐	☐
Appliances	☐	☐	☐
Island	☐	☐	☐

	Good	Average	Poor
Basement	☐	☐	☐
Garage	☐	☐	☐

COMMUNITY

	Good	Average	Poor
Immediate Neighborhood	☐	☐	☐
Close to Employment	☐	☐	☐
Close to Shopping	☐	☐	☐
Close to Transportation	☐	☐	☐
Close to Schools / Daycare	☐	☐	☐
Close to Places of Worship	☐	☐	☐
Near Recreational Facilities	☐	☐	☐
Close to Airport	☐	☐	☐
Near Police and Fire Department	☐	☐	☐

Property Inspection Checklist

PROPERTY DETAILS

BEDROOMS		1	2	3	4
Flooring	Carpet				
	Floorboards				
	Tiles				
	Stained				
	Scratched				
	Cracks				
Walls	Paint				
	Wallpaper				
	Cracks				
	Damp patches				
Windows	Flyscreens				
	Blinds				
	Curtains				
	Lockable				
Balcony					
Ensuite					
Built-in wardrobe					
Air conditioning					
Ceiling fan					
Gas outlet					
TV aerial outlet					
Phone line					
Smoke alarm					
Number of power points					
Dimensions (metres)		x	x	x	x

BATHROOMS		1	2	3
Flooring	Tiles			
	Other			
	Cracks			
Walls	Tiles			
	Paint			
	Wallpaper			
	Cracks			
	Damp patches			
Windows	Flyscreens			
	Blinds			
	Curtains			
	Lockable			
Water pressure	High			
	Medium			
	Low			
Shower	Free standing			
	Over bath			
Bath				
Vanity				
Cupboards				
Towel rails				
Extraction fan				
Heater				
Toilet attached				
Number of power points				

NOTES

Checklist	Good	Average	Poor	Additional Notes
Outdoor Steps and sidewalk				
Outdoor Paint				
Driveway				
Outdoor Plantation				
Outdoor Entry Way				
Indoor Entry Way				
Doors				
Doors Fixtures				
Flooring				
Carpeting				
Windows				
Window Screens				
Window Fixtures				
Window Furnishings				
Ceilings				
Light Fixtures				
Staircases				
Indoor Paint				
Electrical Outlets and Fixtures				
Shelving				
Bedrooms				
Wardrobes and Closets				
Living Room (s)				
Dining Room (s)				
Dens (s)				
Study (s)				
Storage				
Fireplaces				
Bathroom Tiles				
Bathroom Faucets				

Notes:

_____

_____

_____

_____

Address _____ Price _____

Bedrooms _____ Bathrooms _____ Sq.Ft. _____

Lot Size: _____ Year Built _____ School District _____

Annual Tax _____

EXTERIOR

	Good	Average	Poor
View/Yard/Landscaping	☐	☐	☐
Trees	☐	☐	☐
Lawn (Front)	☐	☐	☐
Lawn (Back)	☐	☐	☐
Fences (condition)	☐	☐	☐
Landscaping (condition)	☐	☐	☐
Irrigation / Sprinkler	☐	☐	☐
	☐	☐	☐
House Type	☐	☐	☐
Exterior Siding	☐	☐	☐
Deck / Patio / Porch	☐	☐	☐
Garage	☐	☐	☐
Window / Doors	☐	☐	☐
Roof / Gutters	☐	☐	☐
Fencing	☐	☐	☐

HOME SYSTEMS

	Good	Average	Poor
Electrical	☐	☐	☐
Air Conditioning / Fans	☐	☐	☐
Heating	☐	☐	☐
Security	☐	☐	☐
Plumbing	☐	☐	☐
Intercom	☐	☐	☐

FEATURES

	Good	Average	Poor
Home Warranty	☐	☐	☐
Energy Saving Features	☐	☐	☐

INTERIOR

	Good	Average	Poor
Walls / Trim / Ceilings	☐	☐	☐
Flooring	☐	☐	☐
Stairs	☐	☐	☐
Storage	☐	☐	☐
Living Room	☐	☐	☐
Family Room	☐	☐	☐
Dining Room	☐	☐	☐

	Good	Average	Poor
Master Bedroom	☐	☐	☐
Bedroom 2	☐	☐	☐
Bedroom 3	☐	☐	☐
Bedroom 4	☐	☐	☐
Master Bathroom	☐	☐	☐
Bathroom 2	☐	☐	☐
Bathroom 3	☐	☐	☐
Bonus / Game Room	☐	☐	☐

	Good	Average	Poor
Kitchen	☐	☐	☐
Cabinets	☐	☐	☐
Countertop	☐	☐	☐
Counter Space	☐	☐	☐
Flooring	☐	☐	☐
Oven / Stove	☐	☐	☐
Microwave	☐	☐	☐
Layout	☐	☐	☐
Light Fixtures	☐	☐	☐
Backsplash	☐	☐	☐
Pantry	☐	☐	☐
Appliances	☐	☐	☐
Island	☐	☐	☐

	Good	Average	Poor
Basement	☐	☐	☐
Garage	☐	☐	☐

COMMUNITY

	Good	Average	Poor
Immediate Neighborhood	☐	☐	☐
Close to Employment	☐	☐	☐
Close to Shopping	☐	☐	☐
Close to Transportation	☐	☐	☐
Close to Schools / Daycare	☐	☐	☐
Close to Places of Worship	☐	☐	☐
Near Recreational Facilities	☐	☐	☐
Close to Airport	☐	☐	☐
Near Police and Fire Department	☐	☐	☐

Property Inspection Checklist

PROPERTY DETAILS

BEDROOMS		1	2	3	4	BATHROOMS		1	2	3
Flooring	Carpet					Flooring	Tiles			
	Floorboards						Other			
	Tiles						Cracks			
	Stained					Walls	Tiles			
	Scratched						Paint			
	Cracks						Wallpaper			
Walls	Paint						Cracks			
	Wallpaper						Damp patches			
	Cracks					Windows	Flyscreens			
	Damp patches						Blinds			
Windows	Flyscreens						Curtains			
	Blinds						Lockable			
	Curtains					Water pressure	High			
	Lockable						Medium			
Balcony							Low			
Ensuite						Shower	Free standing			
Built-in wardrobe							Over bath			
Air conditioning						Bath				
Ceiling fan						Vanity				
Gas outlet						Cupboards				
TV aerial outlet						Towel rails				
Phone line						Extraction fan				
Smoke alarm						Heater				
Number of power points						Toilet attached				
Dimensions (metres)		x	x	x	x	Number of power points				

NOTES

Checklist	Good	Average	Poor	Additional Notes
Outdoor Steps and sidewalk				
Outdoor Paint				
Driveway				
Outdoor Plantation				
Outdoor Entry Way				
Indoor Entry Way				
Doors				
Doors Fixtures				
Flooring				
Carpeting				
Windows				
Window Screens				
Window Fixtures				
Window Furnishings				
Ceilings				
Light Fixtures				
Staircases				
Indoor Paint				
Electrical Outlets and Fixtures				
Shelving				
Bedrooms				
Wardrobes and Closets				
Living Room (s)				
Dining Room (s)				
Dens (s)				
Study (s)				
Storage				
Fireplaces				
Bathroom Tiles				
Bathroom Faucets				

Notes:

_____

_____

_____

_____

Address _____ Price _____

Bedrooms _____ Bathrooms _____ Sq.Ft. _____

Lot Size: _____ Year Built _____ School District _____

Annual Tax _____

EXTERIOR

	Good	Average	Poor
View/Yard/Landscaping	☐	☐	☐
Trees	☐	☐	☐
Lawn (Front)	☐	☐	☐
Lawn (Back)	☐	☐	☐
Fences (condition)	☐	☐	☐
Landscaping (condition)	☐	☐	☐
Irrigation / Sprinkler	☐	☐	☐
	☐	☐	☐
House Type	☐	☐	☐
Exterior Siding	☐	☐	☐
Deck / Patio / Porch	☐	☐	☐
Garage	☐	☐	☐
Window / Doors	☐	☐	☐
Roof / Gutters	☐	☐	☐
Fencing	☐	☐	☐

HOME SYSTEMS

	Good	Average	Poor
Electrical	☐	☐	☐
Air Conditioning / Fans	☐	☐	☐
Heating	☐	☐	☐
Security	☐	☐	☐
Plumbing	☐	☐	☐
Intercom	☐	☐	☐

FEATURES

	Good	Average	Poor
Home Warranty	☐	☐	☐
Energy Saving Features	☐	☐	☐

INTERIOR

	Good	Average	Poor
Walls / Trim / Ceilings	☐	☐	☐
Flooring	☐	☐	☐
Stairs	☐	☐	☐
Storage	☐	☐	☐
Living Room	☐	☐	☐
Family Room	☐	☐	☐
Dining Room	☐	☐	☐

	Good	Average	Poor
Master Bedroom	☐	☐	☐
Bedroom 2	☐	☐	☐
Bedroom 3	☐	☐	☐
Bedroom 4	☐	☐	☐
Master Bathroom	☐	☐	☐
Bathroom 2	☐	☐	☐
Bathroom 3	☐	☐	☐
Bonus / Game Room	☐	☐	☐

	Good	Average	Poor
Kitchen	☐	☐	☐
Cabinets	☐	☐	☐
Countertop	☐	☐	☐
Counter Space	☐	☐	☐
Flooring	☐	☐	☐
Oven / Stove	☐	☐	☐
Microwave	☐	☐	☐
Layout	☐	☐	☐
Light Fixtures	☐	☐	☐
Backsplash	☐	☐	☐
Pantry	☐	☐	☐
Appliances	☐	☐	☐
Island	☐	☐	☐

	Good	Average	Poor
Basement	☐	☐	☐
Garage	☐	☐	☐

COMMUNITY

	Good	Average	Poor
Immediate Neighborhood	☐	☐	☐
Close to Employment	☐	☐	☐
Close to Shopping	☐	☐	☐
Close to Transportation	☐	☐	☐
Close to Schools / Daycare	☐	☐	☐
Close to Places of Worship	☐	☐	☐
Near Recreational Facilities	☐	☐	☐
Close to Airport	☐	☐	☐
Near Police and Fire Department	☐	☐	☐

Property Inspection Checklist

PROPERTY DETAILS

BEDROOMS		1	2	3	4
Flooring	Carpet				
	Floorboards				
	Tiles				
	Stained				
	Scratched				
	Cracks				
Walls	Paint				
	Wallpaper				
	Cracks				
	Damp patches				
Windows	Flyscreens				
	Blinds				
	Curtains				
	Lockable				
Balcony					
Ensuite					
Built-in wardrobe					
Air conditioning					
Ceiling fan					
Gas outlet					
TV aerial outlet					
Phone line					
Smoke alarm					
Number of power points					
Dimensions (metres)		X	X	X	X

BATHROOMS		1	2	3
Flooring	Tiles			
	Other			
	Cracks			
Walls	Tiles			
	Paint			
	Wallpaper			
	Cracks			
	Damp patches			
Windows	Flyscreens			
	Blinds			
	Curtains			
	Lockable			
Water pressure	High			
	Medium			
	Low			
Shower	Free standing			
	Over bath			
Bath				
Vanity				
Cupboards				
Towel rails				
Extraction fan				
Heater				
Toilet attached				
Number of power points				

NOTES

Checklist	Good	Average	Poor	Additional Notes
Outdoor Steps and sidewalk				
Outdoor Paint				
Driveway				
Outdoor Plantation				
Outdoor Entry Way				
Indoor Entry Way				
Doors				
Doors Fixtures				
Flooring				
Carpeting				
Windows				
Window Screens				
Window Fixtures				
Window Furnishings				
Ceilings				
Light Fixtures				
Staircases				
Indoor Paint				
Electrical Outlets and Fixtures				
Shelving				
Bedrooms				
Wardrobes and Closets				
Living Room (s)				
Dining Room (s)				
Dens (s)				
Study (s)				
Storage				
Fireplaces				
Bathroom Tiles				
Bathroom Faucets				

Notes:

_____

_____

_____

_____

Address _____ Price _____

Bedrooms _____ Bathrooms _____ Sq.Ft. _____

Lot Size: _____ Year Built _____ School District _____

Annual Tax _____

EXTERIOR

	Good	Average	Poor
View/Yard/Landscaping	☐	☐	☐
Trees	☐	☐	☐
Lawn (Front)	☐	☐	☐
Lawn (Back)	☐	☐	☐
Fences (condition)	☐	☐	☐
Landscaping (condition)	☐	☐	☐
Irrigation / Sprinkler	☐	☐	☐
	☐	☐	☐
House Type	☐	☐	☐
Exterior Siding	☐	☐	☐
Deck / Patio / Porch	☐	☐	☐
Garage	☐	☐	☐
Window / Doors	☐	☐	☐
Roof / Gutters	☐	☐	☐
Fencing	☐	☐	☐

HOME SYSTEMS

	Good	Average	Poor
Electrical	☐	☐	☐
Air Conditioning / Fans	☐	☐	☐
Heating	☐	☐	☐
Security	☐	☐	☐
Plumbing	☐	☐	☐
Intercom	☐	☐	☐

FEATURES

	Good	Average	Poor
Home Warranty	☐	☐	☐
Energy Saving Features	☐	☐	☐

INTERIOR

	Good	Average	Poor
Walls / Trim / Ceilings	☐	☐	☐
Flooring	☐	☐	☐
Stairs	☐	☐	☐
Storage	☐	☐	☐
Living Room	☐	☐	☐
Family Room	☐	☐	☐
Dining Room	☐	☐	☐

	Good	Average	Poor
Master Bedroom	☐	☐	☐
Bedroom 2	☐	☐	☐
Bedroom 3	☐	☐	☐
Bedroom 4	☐	☐	☐
Master Bathroom	☐	☐	☐
Bathroom 2	☐	☐	☐
Bathroom 3	☐	☐	☐
Bonus / Game Room	☐	☐	☐
	Good	Average	Poor
Kitchen	☐	☐	☐
Cabinets	☐	☐	☐
Countertop	☐	☐	☐
Counter Space	☐	☐	☐
Flooring	☐	☐	☐
Oven / Stove	☐	☐	☐
Microwave	☐	☐	☐
Layout	☐	☐	☐
Light Fixtures	☐	☐	☐
Backsplash	☐	☐	☐
Pantry	☐	☐	☐
Appliances	☐	☐	☐
Island	☐	☐	☐
	Good	Average	Poor
Basement	☐	☐	☐
Garage	☐	☐	☐

COMMUNITY

	Good	Average	Poor
Immediate Neighborhood	☐	☐	☐
Close to Employment	☐	☐	☐
Close to Shopping	☐	☐	☐
Close to Transportation	☐	☐	☐
Close to Schools / Daycare	☐	☐	☐
Close to Places of Worship	☐	☐	☐
Near Recreational Facilities	☐	☐	☐
Close to Airport	☐	☐	☐
Near Police and Fire Department	☐	☐	☐

Property Inspection Checklist

PROPERTY DETAILS

BEDROOMS		1	2	3	4
Flooring	Carpet				
	Floorboards				
	Tiles				
	Stained				
	Scratched				
	Cracks				
Walls	Paint				
	Wallpaper				
	Cracks				
	Damp patches				
Windows	Flyscreens				
	Blinds				
	Curtains				
	Lockable				
Balcony					
Ensuite					
Built-in wardrobe					
Air conditioning					
Ceiling fan					
Gas outlet					
TV aerial outlet					
Phone line					
Smoke alarm					
Number of power points					
Dimensions (metres)		x	x	x	x

BATHROOMS		1	2	3
Flooring	Tiles			
	Other			
	Cracks			
Walls	Tiles			
	Paint			
	Wallpaper			
	Cracks			
	Damp patches			
Windows	Flyscreens			
	Blinds			
	Curtains			
	Lockable			
Water pressure	High			
	Medium			
	Low			
Shower	Free standing			
	Over bath			
Bath				
Vanity				
Cupboards				
Towel rails				
Extraction fan				
Heater				
Toilet attached				
Number of power points				

NOTES

Checklist	Good	Average	Poor	Additional Notes
Outdoor Steps and sidewalk				
Outdoor Paint				
Driveway				
Outdoor Plantation				
Outdoor Entry Way				
Indoor Entry Way				
Doors				
Doors Fixtures				
Flooring				
Carpeting				
Windows				
Window Screens				
Window Fixtures				
Window Furnishings				
Ceilings				
Light Fixtures				
Staircases				
Indoor Paint				
Electrical Outlets and Fixtures				
Shelving				
Bedrooms				
Wardrobes and Closets				
Living Room (s)				
Dining Room (s)				
Dens (s)				
Study (s)				
Storage				
Fireplaces				
Bathroom Tiles				
Bathroom Faucets				

Notes:
_____
_____
_____
_____

Address _____ Price _____

Bedrooms _____ Bathrooms _____ Sq.Ft. _____

Lot Size: _____ Year Built _____ School District _____

Annual Tax _____

EXTERIOR

	Good	Average	Poor
View/Yard/Landscaping	☐	☐	☐
Trees	☐	☐	☐
Lawn (Front)	☐	☐	☐
Lawn (Back)	☐	☐	☐
Fences (condition)	☐	☐	☐
Landscaping (condition)	☐	☐	☐
Irrigation / Sprinkler	☐	☐	☐
	☐	☐	☐
House Type	☐	☐	☐
Exterior Siding	☐	☐	☐
Deck / Patio / Porch	☐	☐	☐
Garage	☐	☐	☐
Window / Doors	☐	☐	☐
Roof / Gutters	☐	☐	☐
Fencing	☐	☐	☐

HOME SYSTEMS

	Good	Average	Poor
Electrical	☐	☐	☐
Air Conditioning / Fans	☐	☐	☐
Heating	☐	☐	☐
Security	☐	☐	☐
Plumbing	☐	☐	☐
Intercom	☐	☐	☐

FEATURES

	Good	Average	Poor
Home Warranty	☐	☐	☐
Energy Saving Features	☐	☐	☐

INTERIOR

	Good	Average	Poor
Walls / Trim / Ceilings	☐	☐	☐
Flooring	☐	☐	☐
Stairs	☐	☐	☐
Storage	☐	☐	☐
Living Room	☐	☐	☐
Family Room	☐	☐	☐
Dining Room	☐	☐	☐

	Good	Average	Poor
Master Bedroom	☐	☐	☐
Bedroom 2	☐	☐	☐
Bedroom 3	☐	☐	☐
Bedroom 4	☐	☐	☐
Master Bathroom	☐	☐	☐
Bathroom 2	☐	☐	☐
Bathroom 3	☐	☐	☐
Bonus / Game Room	☐	☐	☐

	Good	Average	Poor
Kitchen	☐	☐	☐
Cabinets	☐	☐	☐
Countertop	☐	☐	☐
Counter Space	☐	☐	☐
Flooring	☐	☐	☐
Oven / Stove	☐	☐	☐
Microwave	☐	☐	☐
Layout	☐	☐	☐
Light Fixtures	☐	☐	☐
Backsplash	☐	☐	☐
Pantry	☐	☐	☐
Appliances	☐	☐	☐
Island	☐	☐	☐

	Good	Average	Poor
Basement	☐	☐	☐
Garage	☐	☐	☐

COMMUNITY

	Good	Average	Poor
Immediate Neighborhood	☐	☐	☐
Close to Employment	☐	☐	☐
Close to Shopping	☐	☐	☐
Close to Transportation	☐	☐	☐
Close to Schools / Daycare	☐	☐	☐
Close to Places of Worship	☐	☐	☐
Near Recreational Facilities	☐	☐	☐
Close to Airport	☐	☐	☐
Near Police and Fire Department	☐	☐	☐

Property Inspection Checklist

PROPERTY DETAILS

BEDROOMS		1	2	3	4
Flooring	Carpet				
	Floorboards				
	Tiles				
	Stained				
	Scratched				
	Cracks				
Walls	Paint				
	Wallpaper				
	Cracks				
	Damp patches				
Windows	Flyscreens				
	Blinds				
	Curtains				
	Lockable				
Balcony					
Ensuite					
Built-in wardrobe					
Air conditioning					
Ceiling fan					
Gas outlet					
TV aerial outlet					
Phone line					
Smoke alarm					
Number of power points					
Dimensions (metres)		X	X	X	X

BATHROOMS		1	2	3
Flooring	Tiles			
	Other			
	Cracks			
Walls	Tiles			
	Paint			
	Wallpaper			
	Cracks			
	Damp patches			
Windows	Flyscreens			
	Blinds			
	Curtains			
	Lockable			
Water pressure	High			
	Medium			
	Low			
Shower	Free standing			
	Over bath			
Bath				
Vanity				
Cupboards				
Towel rails				
Extraction fan				
Heater				
Toilet attached				
Number of power points				

NOTES

Checklist	Good	Average	Poor	Additional Notes
Outdoor Steps and sidewalk				
Outdoor Paint				
Driveway				
Outdoor Plantation				
Outdoor Entry Way				
Indoor Entry Way				
Doors				
Doors Fixtures				
Flooring				
Carpeting				
Windows				
Window Screens				
Window Fixtures				
Window Furnishings				
Ceilings				
Light Fixtures				
Staircases				
Indoor Paint				
Electrical Outlets and Fixtures				
Shelving				
Bedrooms				
Wardrobes and Closets				
Living Room (s)				
Dining Room (s)				
Dens (s)				
Study (s)				
Storage				
Fireplaces				
Bathroom Tiles				
Bathroom Faucets				

Notes:

_____

_____

_____

_____

Address _____   Price _____

Bedrooms _____   Bathrooms _____   Sq.Ft. _____

Lot Size: _____   Year Built _____   School District _____

Annual Tax _____

EXTERIOR

	Good	Average	Poor
View/Yard/Landscaping	☐	☐	☐
Trees	☐	☐	☐
Lawn (Front)	☐	☐	☐
Lawn (Back)	☐	☐	☐
Fences (condition)	☐	☐	☐
Landscaping (condition)	☐	☐	☐
Irrigation / Sprinkler	☐	☐	☐
	☐	☐	☐
House Type	☐	☐	☐
Exterior Siding	☐	☐	☐
Deck / Patio / Porch	☐	☐	☐
Garage	☐	☐	☐
Window / Doors	☐	☐	☐
Roof / Gutters	☐	☐	☐
Fencing	☐	☐	☐

HOME SYSTEMS

	Good	Average	Poor
Electrical	☐	☐	☐
Air Conditioning / Fans	☐	☐	☐
Heating	☐	☐	☐
Security	☐	☐	☐
Plumbing	☐	☐	☐
Intercom	☐	☐	☐

FEATURES

	Good	Average	Poor
Home Warranty	☐	☐	☐
Energy Saving Features	☐	☐	☐

INTERIOR

	Good	Average	Poor
Walls / Trim / Ceilings	☐	☐	☐
Flooring	☐	☐	☐
Stairs	☐	☐	☐
Storage	☐	☐	☐
Living Room	☐	☐	☐
Family Room	☐	☐	☐
Dining Room	☐	☐	☐

	Good	Average	Poor
Master Bedroom	☐	☐	☐
Bedroom 2	☐	☐	☐
Bedroom 3	☐	☐	☐
Bedroom 4	☐	☐	☐
Master Bathroom	☐	☐	☐
Bathroom 2	☐	☐	☐
Bathroom 3	☐	☐	☐
Bonus / Game Room	☐	☐	☐

	Good	Average	Poor
Kitchen	☐	☐	☐
Cabinets	☐	☐	☐
Countertop	☐	☐	☐
Counter Space	☐	☐	☐
Flooring	☐	☐	☐
Oven / Stove	☐	☐	☐
Microwave	☐	☐	☐
Layout	☐	☐	☐
Light Fixtures	☐	☐	☐
Backsplash	☐	☐	☐
Pantry	☐	☐	☐
Appliances	☐	☐	☐
Island	☐	☐	☐

	Good	Average	Poor
Basement	☐	☐	☐
Garage	☐	☐	☐

COMMUNITY

	Good	Average	Poor
Immediate Neighborhood	☐	☐	☐
Close to Employment	☐	☐	☐
Close to Shopping	☐	☐	☐
Close to Transportation	☐	☐	☐
Close to Schools / Daycare	☐	☐	☐
Close to Places of Worship	☐	☐	☐
Near Recreational Facilities	☐	☐	☐
Close to Airport	☐	☐	☐
Near Police and Fire Department	☐	☐	☐

Property Inspection Checklist

PROPERTY DETAILS

BEDROOMS		1	2	3	4
Flooring	Carpet				
	Floorboards				
	Tiles				
	Stained				
	Scratched				
	Cracks				
Walls	Paint				
	Wallpaper				
	Cracks				
	Damp patches				
Windows	Flyscreens				
	Blinds				
	Curtains				
	Lockable				
Balcony					
Ensuite					
Built-in wardrobe					
Air conditioning					
Ceiling fan					
Gas outlet					
TV aerial outlet					
Phone line					
Smoke alarm					
Number of power points					
Dimensions (metres)		x	x	x	x

BATHROOMS		1	2	3
Flooring	Tiles			
	Other			
	Cracks			
Walls	Tiles			
	Paint			
	Wallpaper			
	Cracks			
	Damp patches			
Windows	Flyscreens			
	Blinds			
	Curtains			
	Lockable			
Water pressure	High			
	Medium			
	Low			
Shower	Free standing			
	Over bath			
Bath				
Vanity				
Cupboards				
Towel rails				
Extraction fan				
Heater				
Toilet attached				
Number of power points				

NOTES

Checklist	Good	Average	Poor	Additional Notes
Outdoor Steps and sidewalk				
Outdoor Paint				
Driveway				
Outdoor Plantation				
Outdoor Entry Way				
Indoor Entry Way				
Doors				
Doors Fixtures				
Flooring				
Carpeting				
Windows				
Window Screens				
Window Fixtures				
Window Furnishings				
Ceilings				
Light Fixtures				
Staircases				
Indoor Paint				
Electrical Outlets and Fixtures				
Shelving				
Bedrooms				
Wardrobes and Closets				
Living Room (s)				
Dining Room (s)				
Dens (s)				
Study (s)				
Storage				
Fireplaces				
Bathroom Tiles				
Bathroom Faucets				

Notes:

_____

_____

_____

_____

Address _____ Price _____

Bedrooms _____ Bathrooms _____ Sq.Ft. _____

Lot Size: _____ Year Built _____ School District _____

Annual Tax _____

EXTERIOR

	Good	Average	Poor
View/Yard/Landscaping	☐	☐	☐
Trees	☐	☐	☐
Lawn (Front)	☐	☐	☐
Lawn (Back)	☐	☐	☐
Fences (condition)	☐	☐	☐
Landscaping (condition)	☐	☐	☐
Irrigation / Sprinkler	☐	☐	☐
	☐	☐	☐
House Type	☐	☐	☐
Exterior Siding	☐	☐	☐
Deck / Patio / Porch	☐	☐	☐
Garage	☐	☐	☐
Window / Doors	☐	☐	☐
Roof / Gutters	☐	☐	☐
Fencing	☐	☐	☐

HOME SYSTEMS

	Good	Average	Poor
Electrical	☐	☐	☐
Air Conditioning / Fans	☐	☐	☐
Heating	☐	☐	☐
Security	☐	☐	☐
Plumbing	☐	☐	☐
Intercom	☐	☐	☐

FEATURES

	Good	Average	Poor
Home Warranty	☐	☐	☐
Energy Saving Features	☐	☐	☐

INTERIOR

	Good	Average	Poor
Walls / Trim / Ceilings	☐	☐	☐
Flooring	☐	☐	☐
Stairs	☐	☐	☐
Storage	☐	☐	☐
Living Room	☐	☐	☐
Family Room	☐	☐	☐
Dining Room	☐	☐	☐

	Good	Average	Poor
Master Bedroom	☐	☐	☐
Bedroom 2	☐	☐	☐
Bedroom 3	☐	☐	☐
Bedroom 4	☐	☐	☐
Master Bathroom	☐	☐	☐
Bathroom 2	☐	☐	☐
Bathroom 3	☐	☐	☐
Bonus / Game Room	☐	☐	☐

	Good	Average	Poor
Kitchen	☐	☐	☐
Cabinets	☐	☐	☐
Countertop	☐	☐	☐
Counter Space	☐	☐	☐
Flooring	☐	☐	☐
Oven / Stove	☐	☐	☐
Microwave	☐	☐	☐
Layout	☐	☐	☐
Light Fixtures	☐	☐	☐
Backsplash	☐	☐	☐
Pantry	☐	☐	☐
Appliances	☐	☐	☐
Island	☐	☐	☐

	Good	Average	Poor
Basement	☐	☐	☐
Garage	☐	☐	☐

COMMUNITY

	Good	Average	Poor
Immediate Neighborhood	☐	☐	☐
Close to Employment	☐	☐	☐
Close to Shopping	☐	☐	☐
Close to Transportation	☐	☐	☐
Close to Schools / Daycare	☐	☐	☐
Close to Places of Worship	☐	☐	☐
Near Recreational Facilities	☐	☐	☐
Close to Airport	☐	☐	☐
Near Police and Fire Department	☐	☐	☐

Property Inspection Checklist

PROPERTY DETAILS

BEDROOMS		1	2	3	4
Flooring	Carpet				
	Floorboards				
	Tiles				
	Stained				
	Scratched				
	Cracks				
Walls	Paint				
	Wallpaper				
	Cracks				
	Damp patches				
Windows	Flyscreens				
	Blinds				
	Curtains				
	Lockable				
Balcony					
Ensuite					
Built-in wardrobe					
Air conditioning					
Ceiling fan					
Gas outlet					
TV aerial outlet					
Phone line					
Smoke alarm					
Number of power points					
Dimensions (metres)		x	x	x	x

BATHROOMS		1	2	3
Flooring	Tiles			
	Other			
	Cracks			
Walls	Tiles			
	Paint			
	Wallpaper			
	Cracks			
	Damp patches			
Windows	Flyscreens			
	Blinds			
	Curtains			
	Lockable			
Water pressure	High			
	Medium			
	Low			
Shower	Free standing			
	Over bath			
Bath				
Vanity				
Cupboards				
Towel rails				
Extraction fan				
Heater				
Toilet attached				
Number of power points				

NOTES

Checklist	Good	Average	Poor	Additional Notes
Outdoor Steps and sidewalk				
Outdoor Paint				
Driveway				
Outdoor Plantation				
Outdoor Entry Way				
Indoor Entry Way				
Doors				
Doors Fixtures				
Flooring				
Carpeting				
Windows				
Window Screens				
Window Fixtures				
Window Furnishings				
Ceilings				
Light Fixtures				
Staircases				
Indoor Paint				
Electrical Outlets and Fixtures				
Shelving				
Bedrooms				
Wardrobes and Closets				
Living Room (s)				
Dining Room (s)				
Dens (s)				
Study (s)				
Storage				
Fireplaces				
Bathroom Tiles				
Bathroom Faucets				

Notes:

_____

_____

_____

_____

Address _____ Price _____

Bedrooms _____ Bathrooms _____ Sq.Ft. _____

Lot Size: _____ Year Built _____ School District _____

Annual Tax _____

EXTERIOR

	Good	Average	Poor
View/Yard/Landscaping	☐	☐	☐
Trees	☐	☐	☐
Lawn (Front)	☐	☐	☐
Lawn (Back)	☐	☐	☐
Fences (condition)	☐	☐	☐
Landscaping (condition)	☐	☐	☐
Irrigation / Sprinkler	☐	☐	☐
House Type	☐	☐	☐
Exterior Siding	☐	☐	☐
Deck / Patio / Porch	☐	☐	☐
Garage	☐	☐	☐
Window / Doors	☐	☐	☐
Roof / Gutters	☐	☐	☐
Fencing	☐	☐	☐

HOME SYSTEMS

	Good	Average	Poor
Electrical	☐	☐	☐
Air Conditioning / Fans	☐	☐	☐
Heating	☐	☐	☐
Security	☐	☐	☐
Plumbing	☐	☐	☐
Intercom	☐	☐	☐

FEATURES

	Good	Average	Poor
Home Warranty	☐	☐	☐
Energy Saving Features	☐	☐	☐

INTERIOR

	Good	Average	Poor
Walls / Trim / Ceilings	☐	☐	☐
Flooring	☐	☐	☐
Stairs	☐	☐	☐
Storage	☐	☐	☐
Living Room	☐	☐	☐
Family Room	☐	☐	☐
Dining Room	☐	☐	☐

	Good	Average	Poor
Master Bedroom	☐	☐	☐
Bedroom 2	☐	☐	☐
Bedroom 3	☐	☐	☐
Bedroom 4	☐	☐	☐
Master Bathroom	☐	☐	☐
Bathroom 2	☐	☐	☐
Bathroom 3	☐	☐	☐
Bonus / Game Room	☐	☐	☐

	Good	Average	Poor
Kitchen	☐	☐	☐
Cabinets	☐	☐	☐
Countertop	☐	☐	☐
Counter Space	☐	☐	☐
Flooring	☐	☐	☐
Oven / Stove	☐	☐	☐
Microwave	☐	☐	☐
Layout	☐	☐	☐
Light Fixtures	☐	☐	☐
Backsplash	☐	☐	☐
Pantry	☐	☐	☐
Appliances	☐	☐	☐
Island	☐	☐	☐

	Good	Average	Poor
Basement	☐	☐	☐
Garage	☐	☐	☐

COMMUNITY

	Good	Average	Poor
Immediate Neighborhood	☐	☐	☐
Close to Employment	☐	☐	☐
Close to Shopping	☐	☐	☐
Close to Transportation	☐	☐	☐
Close to Schools / Daycare	☐	☐	☐
Close to Places of Worship	☐	☐	☐
Near Recreational Facilities	☐	☐	☐
Close to Airport	☐	☐	☐
Near Police and Fire Department	☐	☐	☐

Property Inspection Checklist

PROPERTY DETAILS

BEDROOMS		1	2	3	4
Flooring	Carpet				
	Floorboards				
	Tiles				
	Stained				
	Scratched				
	Cracks				
Walls	Paint				
	Wallpaper				
	Cracks				
	Damp patches				
Windows	Flyscreens				
	Blinds				
	Curtains				
	Lockable				
Balcony					
Ensuite					
Built-in wardrobe					
Air conditioning					
Ceiling fan					
Gas outlet					
TV aerial outlet					
Phone line					
Smoke alarm					
Number of power points					
Dimensions (metres)		x	x	x	x

BATHROOMS		1	2	3
Flooring	Tiles			
	Other			
	Cracks			
Walls	Tiles			
	Paint			
	Wallpaper			
	Cracks			
	Damp patches			
Windows	Flyscreens			
	Blinds			
	Curtains			
	Lockable			
Water pressure	High			
	Medium			
	Low			
Shower	Free standing			
	Over bath			
Bath				
Vanity				
Cupboards				
Towel rails				
Extraction fan				
Heater				
Toilet attached				
Number of power points				

NOTES

Checklist	Good	Average	Poor	Additional Notes
Outdoor Steps and sidewalk				
Outdoor Paint				
Driveway				
Outdoor Plantation				
Outdoor Entry Way				
Indoor Entry Way				
Doors				
Doors Fixtures				
Flooring				
Carpeting				
Windows				
Window Screens				
Window Fixtures				
Window Furnishings				
Ceilings				
Light Fixtures				
Staircases				
Indoor Paint				
Electrical Outlets and Fixtures				
Shelving				
Bedrooms				
Wardrobes and Closets				
Living Room (s)				
Dining Room (s)				
Dens (s)				
Study (s)				
Storage				
Fireplaces				
Bathroom Tiles				
Bathroom Faucets				

Notes:

_____

_____

_____

_____

Address _____ Price _____

Bedrooms _____ Bathrooms _____ Sq.Ft. _____

Lot Size: _____ Year Built _____ School District _____

Annual Tax _____

EXTERIOR

	Good	Average	Poor
View/Yard/Landscaping	☐	☐	☐
Trees	☐	☐	☐
Lawn (Front)	☐	☐	☐
Lawn (Back)	☐	☐	☐
Fences (condition)	☐	☐	☐
Landscaping (condition)	☐	☐	☐
Irrigation / Sprinkler	☐	☐	☐
	☐	☐	☐
House Type	☐	☐	☐
Exterior Siding	☐	☐	☐
Deck / Patio / Porch	☐	☐	☐
Garage	☐	☐	☐
Window / Doors	☐	☐	☐
Roof / Gutters	☐	☐	☐
Fencing	☐	☐	☐

HOME SYSTEMS

	Good	Average	Poor
Electrical	☐	☐	☐
Air Conditioning / Fans	☐	☐	☐
Heating	☐	☐	☐
Security	☐	☐	☐
Plumbing	☐	☐	☐
Intercom	☐	☐	☐

FEATURES

	Good	Average	Poor
Home Warranty	☐	☐	☐
Energy Saving Features	☐	☐	☐

INTERIOR

	Good	Average	Poor
Walls / Trim / Ceilings	☐	☐	☐
Flooring	☐	☐	☐
Stairs	☐	☐	☐
Storage	☐	☐	☐
Living Room	☐	☐	☐
Family Room	☐	☐	☐
Dining Room	☐	☐	☐

	Good	Average	Poor
Master Bedroom	☐	☐	☐
Bedroom 2	☐	☐	☐
Bedroom 3	☐	☐	☐
Bedroom 4	☐	☐	☐
Master Bathroom	☐	☐	☐
Bathroom 2	☐	☐	☐
Bathroom 3	☐	☐	☐
Bonus / Game Room	☐	☐	☐

	Good	Average	Poor
Kitchen	☐	☐	☐
Cabinets	☐	☐	☐
Countertop	☐	☐	☐
Counter Space	☐	☐	☐
Flooring	☐	☐	☐
Oven / Stove	☐	☐	☐
Microwave	☐	☐	☐
Layout	☐	☐	☐
Light Fixtures	☐	☐	☐
Backsplash	☐	☐	☐
Pantry	☐	☐	☐
Appliances	☐	☐	☐
Island	☐	☐	☐

	Good	Average	Poor
Basement	☐	☐	☐
Garage	☐	☐	☐

COMMUNITY

	Good	Average	Poor
Immediate Neighborhood	☐	☐	☐
Close to Employment	☐	☐	☐
Close to Shopping	☐	☐	☐
Close to Transportation	☐	☐	☐
Close to Schools / Daycare	☐	☐	☐
Close to Places of Worship	☐	☐	☐
Near Recreational Facilities	☐	☐	☐
Close to Airport	☐	☐	☐
Near Police and Fire Department	☐	☐	☐

Property Inspection Checklist

PROPERTY DETAILS

BEDROOMS		1	2	3	4
Flooring	Carpet				
	Floorboards				
	Tiles				
	Stained				
	Scratched				
	Cracks				
Walls	Paint				
	Wallpaper				
	Cracks				
	Damp patches				
Windows	Flyscreens				
	Blinds				
	Curtains				
	Lockable				
Balcony					
Ensuite					
Built-in wardrobe					
Air conditioning					
Ceiling fan					
Gas outlet					
TV aerial outlet					
Phone line					
Smoke alarm					
Number of power points					
Dimensions (metres)		x	x	x	x

BATHROOMS		1	2	3
Flooring	Tiles			
	Other			
	Cracks			
Walls	Tiles			
	Paint			
	Wallpaper			
	Cracks			
	Damp patches			
Windows	Flyscreens			
	Blinds			
	Curtains			
	Lockable			
Water pressure	High			
	Medium			
	Low			
Shower	Free standing			
	Over bath			
Bath				
Vanity				
Cupboards				
Towel rails				
Extraction fan				
Heater				
Toilet attached				
Number of power points				

NOTES

Checklist	Good	Average	Poor	Additional Notes
Outdoor Steps and sidewalk				
Outdoor Paint				
Driveway				
Outdoor Plantation				
Outdoor Entry Way				
Indoor Entry Way				
Doors				
Doors Fixtures				
Flooring				
Carpeting				
Windows				
Window Screens				
Window Fixtures				
Window Furnishings				
Ceilings				
Light Fixtures				
Staircases				
Indoor Paint				
Electrical Outlets and Fixtures				
Shelving				
Bedrooms				
Wardrobes and Closets				
Living Room (s)				
Dining Room (s)				
Dens (s)				
Study (s)				
Storage				
Fireplaces				
Bathroom Tiles				
Bathroom Faucets				

Notes:
_____
_____
_____
_____

Address _____ Price _____

Bedrooms _____ Bathrooms _____ Sq.Ft. _____

Lot Size: _____ Year Built _____ School District _____

Annual Tax _____

EXTERIOR

	Good	Average	Poor
View/Yard/Landscaping	☐	☐	☐
Trees	☐	☐	☐
Lawn (Front)	☐	☐	☐
Lawn (Back)	☐	☐	☐
Fences (condition)	☐	☐	☐
Landscaping (condition)	☐	☐	☐
Irrigation / Sprinkler	☐	☐	☐
	☐	☐	☐
House Type	☐	☐	☐
Exterior Siding	☐	☐	☐
Deck / Patio / Porch	☐	☐	☐
Garage	☐	☐	☐
Window / Doors	☐	☐	☐
Roof / Gutters	☐	☐	☐
Fencing	☐	☐	☐

HOME SYSTEMS

	Good	Average	Poor
Electrical	☐	☐	☐
Air Conditioning / Fans	☐	☐	☐
Heating	☐	☐	☐
Security	☐	☐	☐
Plumbing	☐	☐	☐
Intercom	☐	☐	☐

FEATURES

	Good	Average	Poor
Home Warranty	☐	☐	☐
Energy Saving Features	☐	☐	☐

INTERIOR

	Good	Average	Poor
Walls / Trim / Ceilings	☐	☐	☐
Flooring	☐	☐	☐
Stairs	☐	☐	☐
Storage	☐	☐	☐
Living Room	☐	☐	☐
Family Room	☐	☐	☐
Dining Room	☐	☐	☐

	Good	Average	Poor
Master Bedroom	☐	☐	☐
Bedroom 2	☐	☐	☐
Bedroom 3	☐	☐	☐
Bedroom 4	☐	☐	☐
Master Bathroom	☐	☐	☐
Bathroom 2	☐	☐	☐
Bathroom 3	☐	☐	☐
Bonus / Game Room	☐	☐	☐

	Good	Average	Poor
Kitchen	☐	☐	☐
Cabinets	☐	☐	☐
Countertop	☐	☐	☐
Counter Space	☐	☐	☐
Flooring	☐	☐	☐
Oven / Stove	☐	☐	☐
Microwave	☐	☐	☐
Layout	☐	☐	☐
Light Fixtures	☐	☐	☐
Backsplash	☐	☐	☐
Pantry	☐	☐	☐
Appliances	☐	☐	☐
Island	☐	☐	☐

	Good	Average	Poor
Basement	☐	☐	☐
Garage	☐	☐	☐

COMMUNITY

	Good	Average	Poor
Immediate Neighborhood	☐	☐	☐
Close to Employment	☐	☐	☐
Close to Shopping	☐	☐	☐
Close to Transportation	☐	☐	☐
Close to Schools / Daycare	☐	☐	☐
Close to Places of Worship	☐	☐	☐
Near Recreational Facilities	☐	☐	☐
Close to Airport	☐	☐	☐
Near Police and Fire Department	☐	☐	☐

Property Inspection Checklist

PROPERTY DETAILS

BEDROOMS		1	2	3	4
Flooring	Carpet				
	Floorboards				
	Tiles				
	Stained				
	Scratched				
	Cracks				
Walls	Paint				
	Wallpaper				
	Cracks				
	Damp patches				
Windows	Flyscreens				
	Blinds				
	Curtains				
	Lockable				
Balcony					
Ensuite					
Built-in wardrobe					
Air conditioning					
Ceiling fan					
Gas outlet					
TV aerial outlet					
Phone line					
Smoke alarm					
Number of power points					
Dimensions (metres)		x	x	x	x

BATHROOMS		1	2	3
Flooring	Tiles			
	Other			
	Cracks			
Walls	Tiles			
	Paint			
	Wallpaper			
	Cracks			
	Damp patches			
Windows	Flyscreens			
	Blinds			
	Curtains			
	Lockable			
Water pressure	High			
	Medium			
	Low			
Shower	Free standing			
	Over bath			
Bath				
Vanity				
Cupboards				
Towel rails				
Extraction fan				
Heater				
Toilet attached				
Number of power points				

NOTES

Checklist	Good	Average	Poor	Additional Notes
Outdoor Steps and sidewalk				
Outdoor Paint				
Driveway				
Outdoor Plantation				
Outdoor Entry Way				
Indoor Entry Way				
Doors				
Doors Fixtures				
Flooring				
Carpeting				
Windows				
Window Screens				
Window Fixtures				
Window Furnishings				
Ceilings				
Light Fixtures				
Staircases				
Indoor Paint				
Electrical Outlets and Fixtures				
Shelving				
Bedrooms				
Wardrobes and Closets				
Living Room (s)				
Dining Room (s)				
Dens (s)				
Study (s)				
Storage				
Fireplaces				
Bathroom Tiles				
Bathroom Faucets				

Notes:

_____

_____

_____

_____

Address _____ Price _____

Bedrooms _____ Bathrooms _____ Sq.Ft. _____

Lot Size: _____ Year Built _____ School District _____

Annual Tax _____

EXTERIOR

	Good	Average	Poor
View/Yard/Landscaping	☐	☐	☐
Trees	☐	☐	☐
Lawn (Front)	☐	☐	☐
Lawn (Back)	☐	☐	☐
Fences (condition)	☐	☐	☐
Landscaping (condition)	☐	☐	☐
Irrigation / Sprinkler	☐	☐	☐
	☐	☐	☐
House Type	☐	☐	☐
Exterior Siding	☐	☐	☐
Deck / Patio / Porch	☐	☐	☐
Garage	☐	☐	☐
Window / Doors	☐	☐	☐
Roof / Gutters	☐	☐	☐
Fencing	☐	☐	☐

HOME SYSTEMS

	Good	Average	Poor
Electrical	☐	☐	☐
Air Conditioning / Fans	☐	☐	☐
Heating	☐	☐	☐
Security	☐	☐	☐
Plumbing	☐	☐	☐
Intercom	☐	☐	☐

FEATURES

	Good	Average	Poor
Home Warranty	☐	☐	☐
Energy Saving Features	☐	☐	☐

INTERIOR

	Good	Average	Poor
Walls / Trim / Ceilings	☐	☐	☐
Flooring	☐	☐	☐
Stairs	☐	☐	☐
Storage	☐	☐	☐
Living Room	☐	☐	☐
Family Room	☐	☐	☐
Dining Room	☐	☐	☐

	Good	Average	Poor
Master Bedroom	☐	☐	☐
Bedroom 2	☐	☐	☐
Bedroom 3	☐	☐	☐
Bedroom 4	☐	☐	☐
Master Bathroom	☐	☐	☐
Bathroom 2	☐	☐	☐
Bathroom 3	☐	☐	☐
Bonus / Game Room	☐	☐	☐

	Good	Average	Poor
Kitchen	☐	☐	☐
Cabinets	☐	☐	☐
Countertop	☐	☐	☐
Counter Space	☐	☐	☐
Flooring	☐	☐	☐
Oven / Stove	☐	☐	☐
Microwave	☐	☐	☐
Layout	☐	☐	☐
Light Fixtures	☐	☐	☐
Backsplash	☐	☐	☐
Pantry	☐	☐	☐
Appliances	☐	☐	☐
Island	☐	☐	☐

	Good	Average	Poor
Basement	☐	☐	☐
Garage	☐	☐	☐

COMMUNITY

	Good	Average	Poor
Immediate Neighborhood	☐	☐	☐
Close to Employment	☐	☐	☐
Close to Shopping	☐	☐	☐
Close to Transportation	☐	☐	☐
Close to Schools / Daycare	☐	☐	☐
Close to Places of Worship	☐	☐	☐
Near Recreational Facilities	☐	☐	☐
Close to Airport	☐	☐	☐
Near Police and Fire Department	☐	☐	☐

Property Inspection Checklist

PROPERTY DETAILS

BEDROOMS		1	2	3	4
Flooring	Carpet				
	Floorboards				
	Tiles				
	Stained				
	Scratched				
	Cracks				
Walls	Paint				
	Wallpaper				
	Cracks				
	Damp patches				
Windows	Flyscreens				
	Blinds				
	Curtains				
	Lockable				
Balcony					
Ensuite					
Built-in wardrobe					
Air conditioning					
Ceiling fan					
Gas outlet					
TV aerial outlet					
Phone line					
Smoke alarm					
Number of power points					
Dimensions (metres)		x	x	x	x

BATHROOMS		1	2	3
Flooring	Tiles			
	Other			
	Cracks			
Walls	Tiles			
	Paint			
	Wallpaper			
	Cracks			
	Damp patches			
Windows	Flyscreens			
	Blinds			
	Curtains			
	Lockable			
Water pressure	High			
	Medium			
	Low			
Shower	Free standing			
	Over bath			
Bath				
Vanity				
Cupboards				
Towel rails				
Extraction fan				
Heater				
Toilet attached				
Number of power points				

NOTES

Checklist	Good	Average	Poor	Additional Notes
Outdoor Steps and sidewalk				
Outdoor Paint				
Driveway				
Outdoor Plantation				
Outdoor Entry Way				
Indoor Entry Way				
Doors				
Doors Fixtures				
Flooring				
Carpeting				
Windows				
Window Screens				
Window Fixtures				
Window Furnishings				
Ceilings				
Light Fixtures				
Staircases				
Indoor Paint				
Electrical Outlets and Fixtures				
Shelving				
Bedrooms				
Wardrobes and Closets				
Living Room (s)				
Dining Room (s)				
Dens (s)				
Study (s)				
Storage				
Fireplaces				
Bathroom Tiles				
Bathroom Faucets				

Notes:

_____

_____

_____

_____

Address _____ Price _____

Bedrooms _____ Bathrooms _____ Sq.Ft. _____

Lot Size: _____ Year Built _____ School District _____

Annual Tax _____

EXTERIOR

	Good	Average	Poor
View/Yard/Landscaping	☐	☐	☐
Trees	☐	☐	☐
Lawn (Front)	☐	☐	☐
Lawn (Back)	☐	☐	☐
Fences (condition)	☐	☐	☐
Landscaping (condition)	☐	☐	☐
Irrigation / Sprinkler	☐	☐	☐
	☐	☐	☐
House Type	☐	☐	☐
Exterior Siding	☐	☐	☐
Deck / Patio / Porch	☐	☐	☐
Garage	☐	☐	☐
Window / Doors	☐	☐	☐
Roof / Gutters	☐	☐	☐
Fencing	☐	☐	☐

HOME SYSTEMS

	Good	Average	Poor
Electrical	☐	☐	☐
Air Conditioning / Fans	☐	☐	☐
Heating	☐	☐	☐
Security	☐	☐	☐
Plumbing	☐	☐	☐
Intercom	☐	☐	☐

FEATURES

	Good	Average	Poor
Home Warranty	☐	☐	☐
Energy Saving Features	☐	☐	☐

INTERIOR

	Good	Average	Poor
Walls / Trim / Ceilings	☐	☐	☐
Flooring	☐	☐	☐
Stairs	☐	☐	☐
Storage	☐	☐	☐
Living Room	☐	☐	☐
Family Room	☐	☐	☐
Dining Room	☐	☐	☐

	Good	Average	Poor
Master Bedroom	☐	☐	☐
Bedroom 2	☐	☐	☐
Bedroom 3	☐	☐	☐
Bedroom 4	☐	☐	☐
Master Bathroom	☐	☐	☐
Bathroom 2	☐	☐	☐
Bathroom 3	☐	☐	☐
Bonus / Game Room	☐	☐	☐

	Good	Average	Poor
Kitchen	☐	☐	☐
Cabinets	☐	☐	☐
Countertop	☐	☐	☐
Counter Space	☐	☐	☐
Flooring	☐	☐	☐
Oven / Stove	☐	☐	☐
Microwave	☐	☐	☐
Layout	☐	☐	☐
Light Fixtures	☐	☐	☐
Backsplash	☐	☐	☐
Pantry	☐	☐	☐
Appliances	☐	☐	☐
Island	☐	☐	☐

	Good	Average	Poor
Basement	☐	☐	☐
Garage	☐	☐	☐

COMMUNITY

	Good	Average	Poor
Immediate Neighborhood	☐	☐	☐
Close to Employment	☐	☐	☐
Close to Shopping	☐	☐	☐
Close to Transportation	☐	☐	☐
Close to Schools / Daycare	☐	☐	☐
Close to Places of Worship	☐	☐	☐
Near Recreational Facilities	☐	☐	☐
Close to Airport	☐	☐	☐
Near Police and Fire Department	☐	☐	☐

Property Inspection Checklist

PROPERTY DETAILS

BEDROOMS		1	2	3	4
Flooring	Carpet				
	Floorboards				
	Tiles				
	Stained				
	Scratched				
	Cracks				
Walls	Paint				
	Wallpaper				
	Cracks				
	Damp patches				
Windows	Flyscreens				
	Blinds				
	Curtains				
	Lockable				
Balcony					
Ensuite					
Built-in wardrobe					
Air conditioning					
Ceiling fan					
Gas outlet					
TV aerial outlet					
Phone line					
Smoke alarm					
Number of power points					
Dimensions (metres)		x	x	x	x

BATHROOMS		1	2	3
Flooring	Tiles			
	Other			
	Cracks			
Walls	Tiles			
	Paint			
	Wallpaper			
	Cracks			
	Damp patches			
Windows	Flyscreens			
	Blinds			
	Curtains			
	Lockable			
Water pressure	High			
	Medium			
	Low			
Shower	Free standing			
	Over bath			
Bath				
Vanity				
Cupboards				
Towel rails				
Extraction fan				
Heater				
Toilet attached				
Number of power points				

NOTES

Checklist	Good	Average	Poor	Additional Notes
Outdoor Steps and sidewalk				
Outdoor Paint				
Driveway				
Outdoor Plantation				
Outdoor Entry Way				
Indoor Entry Way				
Doors				
Doors Fixtures				
Flooring				
Carpeting				
Windows				
Window Screens				
Window Fixtures				
Window Furnishings				
Ceilings				
Light Fixtures				
Staircases				
Indoor Paint				
Electrical Outlets and Fixtures				
Shelving				
Bedrooms				
Wardrobes and Closets				
Living Room (s)				
Dining Room (s)				
Dens (s)				
Study (s)				
Storage				
Fireplaces				
Bathroom Tiles				
Bathroom Faucets				

Notes:

_____

_____

_____

_____

Address _____ Price _____

Bedrooms _____ Bathrooms _____ Sq.Ft. _____

Lot Size: _____ Year Built _____ School District _____

Annual Tax _____

EXTERIOR

	Good	Average	Poor
View/Yard/Landscaping	☐	☐	☐
Trees	☐	☐	☐
Lawn (Front)	☐	☐	☐
Lawn (Back)	☐	☐	☐
Fences (condition)	☐	☐	☐
Landscaping (condition)	☐	☐	☐
Irrigation / Sprinkler	☐	☐	☐
	☐	☐	☐
House Type	☐	☐	☐
Exterior Siding	☐	☐	☐
Deck / Patio / Porch	☐	☐	☐
Garage	☐	☐	☐
Window / Doors	☐	☐	☐
Roof / Gutters	☐	☐	☐
Fencing	☐	☐	☐

HOME SYSTEMS

	Good	Average	Poor
Electrical	☐	☐	☐
Air Conditioning / Fans	☐	☐	☐
Heating	☐	☐	☐
Security	☐	☐	☐
Plumbing	☐	☐	☐
Intercom	☐	☐	☐

FEATURES

	Good	Average	Poor
Home Warranty	☐	☐	☐
Energy Saving Features	☐	☐	☐

INTERIOR

	Good	Average	Poor
Walls / Trim / Ceilings	☐	☐	☐
Flooring	☐	☐	☐
Stairs	☐	☐	☐
Storage	☐	☐	☐
Living Room	☐	☐	☐
Family Room	☐	☐	☐
Dining Room	☐	☐	☐

	Good	Average	Poor
Master Bedroom	☐	☐	☐
Bedroom 2	☐	☐	☐
Bedroom 3	☐	☐	☐
Bedroom 4	☐	☐	☐
Master Bathroom	☐	☐	☐
Bathroom 2	☐	☐	☐
Bathroom 3	☐	☐	☐
Bonus / Game Room	☐	☐	☐

	Good	Average	Poor
Kitchen	☐	☐	☐
Cabinets	☐	☐	☐
Countertop	☐	☐	☐
Counter Space	☐	☐	☐
Flooring	☐	☐	☐
Oven / Stove	☐	☐	☐
Microwave	☐	☐	☐
Layout	☐	☐	☐
Light Fixtures	☐	☐	☐
Backsplash	☐	☐	☐
Pantry	☐	☐	☐
Appliances	☐	☐	☐
Island	☐	☐	☐

	Good	Average	Poor
Basement	☐	☐	☐
Garage	☐	☐	☐

COMMUNITY

	Good	Average	Poor
Immediate Neighborhood	☐	☐	☐
Close to Employment	☐	☐	☐
Close to Shopping	☐	☐	☐
Close to Transportation	☐	☐	☐
Close to Schools / Daycare	☐	☐	☐
Close to Places of Worship	☐	☐	☐
Near Recreational Facilities	☐	☐	☐
Close to Airport	☐	☐	☐
Near Police and Fire Department	☐	☐	☐

Property Inspection Checklist

PROPERTY DETAILS

BEDROOMS		1	2	3	4
Flooring	Carpet				
	Floorboards				
	Tiles				
	Stained				
	Scratched				
	Cracks				
Walls	Paint				
	Wallpaper				
	Cracks				
	Damp patches				
Windows	Flyscreens				
	Blinds				
	Curtains				
	Lockable				
Balcony					
Ensuite					
Built-in wardrobe					
Air conditioning					
Ceiling fan					
Gas outlet					
TV aerial outlet					
Phone line					
Smoke alarm					
Number of power points					
Dimensions (metres)		X	X	X	X

BATHROOMS		1	2	3
Flooring	Tiles			
	Other			
	Cracks			
Walls	Tiles			
	Paint			
	Wallpaper			
	Cracks			
	Damp patches			
Windows	Flyscreens			
	Blinds			
	Curtains			
	Lockable			
Water pressure	High			
	Medium			
	Low			
Shower	Free standing			
	Over bath			
Bath				
Vanity				
Cupboards				
Towel rails				
Extraction fan				
Heater				
Toilet attached				
Number of power points				

NOTES

Checklist	Good	Average	Poor	Additional Notes
Outdoor Steps and sidewalk				
Outdoor Paint				
Driveway				
Outdoor Plantation				
Outdoor Entry Way				
Indoor Entry Way				
Doors				
Doors Fixtures				
Flooring				
Carpeting				
Windows				
Window Screens				
Window Fixtures				
Window Furnishings				
Ceilings				
Light Fixtures				
Staircases				
Indoor Paint				
Electrical Outlets and Fixtures				
Shelving				
Bedrooms				
Wardrobes and Closets				
Living Room (s)				
Dining Room (s)				
Dens (s)				
Study (s)				
Storage				
Fireplaces				
Bathroom Tiles				
Bathroom Faucets				

Notes:

_____

_____

_____

_____

Address _____ Price _____

Bedrooms _____ Bathrooms _____ Sq.Ft. _____

Lot Size: _____ Year Built _____ School District _____

Annual Tax _____

EXTERIOR

	Good	Average	Poor
View/Yard/Landscaping	☐	☐	☐
Trees	☐	☐	☐
Lawn (Front)	☐	☐	☐
Lawn (Back)	☐	☐	☐
Fences (condition)	☐	☐	☐
Landscaping (condition)	☐	☐	☐
Irrigation / Sprinkler	☐	☐	☐
	☐	☐	☐
House Type	☐	☐	☐
Exterior Siding	☐	☐	☐
Deck / Patio / Porch	☐	☐	☐
Garage	☐	☐	☐
Window / Doors	☐	☐	☐
Roof / Gutters	☐	☐	☐
Fencing	☐	☐	☐

HOME SYSTEMS

	Good	Average	Poor
Electrical	☐	☐	☐
Air Conditioning / Fans	☐	☐	☐
Heating	☐	☐	☐
Security	☐	☐	☐
Plumbing	☐	☐	☐
Intercom	☐	☐	☐

FEATURES

	Good	Average	Poor
Home Warranty	☐	☐	☐
Energy Saving Features	☐	☐	☐

INTERIOR

	Good	Average	Poor
Walls / Trim / Ceilings	☐	☐	☐
Flooring	☐	☐	☐
Stairs	☐	☐	☐
Storage	☐	☐	☐
Living Room	☐	☐	☐
Family Room	☐	☐	☐
Dining Room	☐	☐	☐

	Good	Average	Poor
Master Bedroom	☐	☐	☐
Bedroom 2	☐	☐	☐
Bedroom 3	☐	☐	☐
Bedroom 4	☐	☐	☐
Master Bathroom	☐	☐	☐
Bathroom 2	☐	☐	☐
Bathroom 3	☐	☐	☐
Bonus / Game Room	☐	☐	☐

	Good	Average	Poor
Kitchen	☐	☐	☐
Cabinets	☐	☐	☐
Countertop	☐	☐	☐
Counter Space	☐	☐	☐
Flooring	☐	☐	☐
Oven / Stove	☐	☐	☐
Microwave	☐	☐	☐
Layout	☐	☐	☐
Light Fixtures	☐	☐	☐
Backsplash	☐	☐	☐
Pantry	☐	☐	☐
Appliances	☐	☐	☐
Island	☐	☐	☐

	Good	Average	Poor
Basement	☐	☐	☐
Garage	☐	☐	☐

COMMUNITY

	Good	Average	Poor
Immediate Neighborhood	☐	☐	☐
Close to Employment	☐	☐	☐
Close to Shopping	☐	☐	☐
Close to Transportation	☐	☐	☐
Close to Schools / Daycare	☐	☐	☐
Close to Places of Worship	☐	☐	☐
Near Recreational Facilities	☐	☐	☐
Close to Airport	☐	☐	☐
Near Police and Fire Department	☐	☐	☐

Property Inspection Checklist

PROPERTY DETAILS

BEDROOMS		1	2	3	4	BATHROOMS		1	2	3
Flooring	Carpet					Flooring	Tiles			
	Floorboards						Other			
	Tiles						Cracks			
	Stained					Walls	Tiles			
	Scratched						Paint			
	Cracks						Wallpaper			
Walls	Paint						Cracks			
	Wallpaper						Damp patches			
	Cracks					Windows	Flyscreens			
	Damp patches						Blinds			
Windows	Flyscreens						Curtains			
	Blinds						Lockable			
	Curtains					Water pressure	High			
	Lockable						Medium			
Balcony							Low			
Ensuite						Shower	Free standing			
Built-in wardrobe							Over bath			
Air conditioning						Bath				
Ceiling fan						Vanity				
Gas outlet						Cupboards				
TV aerial outlet						Towel rails				
Phone line						Extraction fan		♭		
Smoke alarm						Heater				
Number of power points						Toilet attached				
Dimensions (metres)		x	x	x	x	Number of power points				

NOTES

Checklist	Good	Average	Poor	Additional Notes
Outdoor Steps and sidewalk				
Outdoor Paint				
Driveway				
Outdoor Plantation				
Outdoor Entry Way				
Indoor Entry Way				
Doors				
Doors Fixtures				
Flooring				
Carpeting				
Windows				
Window Screens				
Window Fixtures				
Window Furnishings				
Ceilings				
Light Fixtures				
Staircases				
Indoor Paint				
Electrical Outlets and Fixtures				
Shelving				
Bedrooms				
Wardrobes and Closets				
Living Room (s)				
Dining Room (s)				
Dens (s)				
Study (s)				
Storage				
Fireplaces				
Bathroom Tiles				
Bathroom Faucets				

Notes:

_____

_____

_____

_____

Address _____ Price _____

Bedrooms _____ Bathrooms _____ Sq.Ft. _____

Lot Size: _____ Year Built _____ School District _____

Annual Tax _____

EXTERIOR

	Good	Average	Poor
View/Yard/Landscaping	☐	☐	☐
Trees	☐	☐	☐
Lawn (Front)	☐	☐	☐
Lawn (Back)	☐	☐	☐
Fences (condition)	☐	☐	☐
Landscaping (condition)	☐	☐	☐
Irrigation / Sprinkler	☐	☐	☐
	☐	☐	☐
House Type	☐	☐	☐
Exterior Siding	☐	☐	☐
Deck / Patio / Porch	☐	☐	☐
Garage	☐	☐	☐
Window / Doors	☐	☐	☐
Roof / Gutters	☐	☐	☐
Fencing	☐	☐	☐

HOME SYSTEMS

	Good	Average	Poor
Electrical	☐	☐	☐
Air Conditioning / Fans	☐	☐	☐
Heating	☐	☐	☐
Security	☐	☐	☐
Plumbing	☐	☐	☐
Intercom	☐	☐	☐

FEATURES

	Good	Average	Poor
Home Warranty	☐	☐	☐
Energy Saving Features	☐	☐	☐

INTERIOR

	Good	Average	Poor
Walls / Trim / Ceilings	☐	☐	☐
Flooring	☐	☐	☐
Stairs	☐	☐	☐
Storage	☐	☐	☐
Living Room	☐	☐	☐
Family Room	☐	☐	☐
Dining Room	☐	☐	☐

	Good	Average	Poor
Master Bedroom	☐	☐	☐
Bedroom 2	☐	☐	☐
Bedroom 3	☐	☐	☐
Bedroom 4	☐	☐	☐
Master Bathroom	☐	☐	☐
Bathroom 2	☐	☐	☐
Bathroom 3	☐	☐	☐
Bonus / Game Room	☐	☐	☐

	Good	Average	Poor
Kitchen	☐	☐	☐
Cabinets	☐	☐	☐
Countertop	☐	☐	☐
Counter Space	☐	☐	☐
Flooring	☐	☐	☐
Oven / Stove	☐	☐	☐
Microwave	☐	☐	☐
Layout	☐	☐	☐
Light Fixtures	☐	☐	☐
Backsplash	☐	☐	☐
Pantry	☐	☐	☐
Appliances	☐	☐	☐
Island	☐	☐	☐

	Good	Average	Poor
Basement	☐	☐	☐
Garage	☐	☐	☐

COMMUNITY

	Good	Average	Poor
Immediate Neighborhood	☐	☐	☐
Close to Employment	☐	☐	☐
Close to Shopping	☐	☐	☐
Close to Transportation	☐	☐	☐
Close to Schools / Daycare	☐	☐	☐
Close to Places of Worship	☐	☐	☐
Near Recreational Facilities	☐	☐	☐
Close to Airport	☐	☐	☐
Near Police and Fire Department	☐	☐	☐

Property Inspection Checklist

PROPERTY DETAILS

BEDROOMS		1	2	3	4
Flooring	Carpet				
	Floorboards				
	Tiles				
	Stained				
	Scratched				
	Cracks				
Walls	Paint				
	Wallpaper				
	Cracks				
	Damp patches				
Windows	Flyscreens				
	Blinds				
	Curtains				
	Lockable				
Balcony					
Ensuite					
Built-in wardrobe					
Air conditioning					
Ceiling fan					
Gas outlet					
TV aerial outlet					
Phone line					
Smoke alarm					
Number of power points					
Dimensions (metres)		x	x	x	x

BATHROOMS		1	2	3
Flooring	Tiles			
	Other			
	Cracks			
Walls	Tiles			
	Paint			
	Wallpaper			
	Cracks			
	Damp patches			
Windows	Flyscreens			
	Blinds			
	Curtains			
	Lockable			
Water pressure	High			
	Medium			
	Low			
Shower	Free standing			
	Over bath			
Bath				
Vanity				
Cupboards				
Towel rails				
Extraction fan				
Heater				
Toilet attached				
Number of power points				

NOTES

Checklist	Good	Average	Poor	Additional Notes
Outdoor Steps and sidewalk				
Outdoor Paint				
Driveway				
Outdoor Plantation				
Outdoor Entry Way				
Indoor Entry Way				
Doors				
Doors Fixtures				
Flooring				
Carpeting				
Windows				
Window Screens				
Window Fixtures				
Window Furnishings				
Ceilings				
Light Fixtures				
Staircases				
Indoor Paint				
Electrical Outlets and Fixtures				
Shelving				
Bedrooms				
Wardrobes and Closets				
Living Room (s)				
Dining Room (s)				
Dens (s)				
Study (s)				
Storage				
Fireplaces				
Bathroom Tiles				
Bathroom Faucets				

Notes:

_____

_____

_____

_____

Address _____ Price _____

Bedrooms _____ Bathrooms _____ Sq.Ft. _____

Lot Size: _____ Year Built _____ School District _____

Annual Tax _____

EXTERIOR

	Good	Average	Poor
View/Yard/Landscaping	☐	☐	☐
Trees	☐	☐	☐
Lawn (Front)	☐	☐	☐
Lawn (Back)	☐	☐	☐
Fences (condition)	☐	☐	☐
Landscaping (condition)	☐	☐	☐
Irrigation / Sprinkler	☐	☐	☐
	☐	☐	☐
House Type	☐	☐	☐
Exterior Siding	☐	☐	☐
Deck / Patio / Porch	☐	☐	☐
Garage	☐	☐	☐
Window / Doors	☐	☐	☐
Roof / Gutters	☐	☐	☐
Fencing	☐	☐	☐

HOME SYSTEMS

	Good	Average	Poor
Electrical	☐	☐	☐
Air Conditioning / Fans	☐	☐	☐
Heating	☐	☐	☐
Security	☐	☐	☐
Plumbing	☐	☐	☐
Intercom	☐	☐	☐

FEATURES

	Good	Average	Poor
Home Warranty	☐	☐	☐
Energy Saving Features	☐	☐	☐

INTERIOR

	Good	Average	Poor
Walls / Trim / Ceilings	☐	☐	☐
Flooring	☐	☐	☐
Stairs	☐	☐	☐
Storage	☐	☐	☐
Living Room	☐	☐	☐
Family Room	☐	☐	☐
Dining Room	☐	☐	☐

	Good	Average	Poor
Master Bedroom	☐	☐	☐
Bedroom 2	☐	☐	☐
Bedroom 3	☐	☐	☐
Bedroom 4	☐	☐	☐
Master Bathroom	☐	☐	☐
Bathroom 2	☐	☐	☐
Bathroom 3	☐	☐	☐
Bonus / Game Room	☐	☐	☐

	Good	Average	Poor
Kitchen	☐	☐	☐
Cabinets	☐	☐	☐
Countertop	☐	☐	☐
Counter Space	☐	☐	☐
Flooring	☐	☐	☐
Oven / Stove	☐	☐	☐
Microwave	☐	☐	☐
Layout	☐	☐	☐
Light Fixtures	☐	☐	☐
Backsplash	☐	☐	☐
Pantry	☐	☐	☐
Appliances	☐	☐	☐
Island	☐	☐	☐

	Good	Average	Poor
Basement	☐	☐	☐
Garage	☐	☐	☐

COMMUNITY

	Good	Average	Poor
Immediate Neighborhood	☐	☐	☐
Close to Employment	☐	☐	☐
Close to Shopping	☐	☐	☐
Close to Transportation	☐	☐	☐
Close to Schools / Daycare	☐	☐	☐
Close to Places of Worship	☐	☐	☐
Near Recreational Facilities	☐	☐	☐
Close to Airport	☐	☐	☐
Near Police and Fire Department	☐	☐	☐

Property Inspection Checklist

PROPERTY DETAILS

BEDROOMS		1	2	3	4
Flooring	Carpet				
	Floorboards				
	Tiles				
	Stained				
	Scratched				
	Cracks				
Walls	Paint				
	Wallpaper				
	Cracks				
	Damp patches				
Windows	Flyscreens				
	Blinds				
	Curtains				
	Lockable				
Balcony					
Ensuite					
Built-in wardrobe					
Air conditioning					
Ceiling fan					
Gas outlet					
TV aerial outlet					
Phone line					
Smoke alarm					
Number of power points					
Dimensions (metres)		x	x	x	x

BATHROOMS		1	2	3
Flooring	Tiles			
	Other			
	Cracks			
Walls	Tiles			
	Paint			
	Wallpaper			
	Cracks			
	Damp patches			
Windows	Flyscreens			
	Blinds			
	Curtains			
	Lockable			
Water pressure	High			
	Medium			
	Low			
Shower	Free standing			
	Over bath			
Bath				
Vanity				
Cupboards				
Towel rails				
Extraction fan				
Heater				
Toilet attached				
Number of power points				

NOTES

Checklist	Good	Average	Poor	Additional Notes
Outdoor Steps and sidewalk				
Outdoor Paint				
Driveway				
Outdoor Plantation				
Outdoor Entry Way				
Indoor Entry Way				
Doors				
Doors Fixtures				
Flooring				
Carpeting				
Windows				
Window Screens				
Window Fixtures				
Window Furnishings				
Ceilings				
Light Fixtures				
Staircases				
Indoor Paint				
Electrical Outlets and Fixtures				
Shelving				
Bedrooms				
Wardrobes and Closets				
Living Room (s)				
Dining Room (s)				
Dens (s)				
Study (s)				
Storage				
Fireplaces				
Bathroom Tiles				
Bathroom Faucets				

Notes:

_____

_____

_____

_____

Address _____ Price _____

Bedrooms _____ Bathrooms _____ Sq.Ft. _____

Lot Size: _____ Year Built _____ School District _____

Annual Tax _____

EXTERIOR

	Good	Average	Poor
View/Yard/Landscaping	☐	☐	☐
Trees	☐	☐	☐
Lawn (Front)	☐	☐	☐
Lawn (Back)	☐	☐	☐
Fences (condition)	☐	☐	☐
Landscaping (condition)	☐	☐	☐
Irrigation / Sprinkler	☐	☐	☐
	☐	☐	☐
House Type	☐	☐	☐
Exterior Siding	☐	☐	☐
Deck / Patio / Porch	☐	☐	☐
Garage	☐	☐	☐
Window / Doors	☐	☐	☐
Roof / Gutters	☐	☐	☐
Fencing	☐	☐	☐

HOME SYSTEMS

	Good	Average	Poor
Electrical	☐	☐	☐
Air Conditioning / Fans	☐	☐	☐
Heating	☐	☐	☐
Security	☐	☐	☐
Plumbing	☐	☐	☐
Intercom	☐	☐	☐

FEATURES

	Good	Average	Poor
Home Warranty	☐	☐	☐
Energy Saving Features	☐	☐	☐

INTERIOR

	Good	Average	Poor
Walls / Trim / Ceilings	☐	☐	☐
Flooring	☐	☐	☐
Stairs	☐	☐	☐
Storage	☐	☐	☐
Living Room	☐	☐	☐
Family Room	☐	☐	☐
Dining Room	☐	☐	☐

	Good	Average	Poor
Master Bedroom	☐	☐	☐
Bedroom 2	☐	☐	☐
Bedroom 3	☐	☐	☐
Bedroom 4	☐	☐	☐
Master Bathroom	☐	☐	☐
Bathroom 2	☐	☐	☐
Bathroom 3	☐	☐	☐
Bonus / Game Room	☐	☐	☐

	Good	Average	Poor
Kitchen	☐	☐	☐
Cabinets	☐	☐	☐
Countertop	☐	☐	☐
Counter Space	☐	☐	☐
Flooring	☐	☐	☐
Oven / Stove	☐	☐	☐
Microwave	☐	☐	☐
Layout	☐	☐	☐
Light Fixtures	☐	☐	☐
Backsplash	☐	☐	☐
Pantry	☐	☐	☐
Appliances	☐	☐	☐
Island	☐	☐	☐

	Good	Average	Poor
Basement	☐	☐	☐
Garage	☐	☐	☐

COMMUNITY

	Good	Average	Poor
Immediate Neighborhood	☐	☐	☐
Close to Employment	☐	☐	☐
Close to Shopping	☐	☐	☐
Close to Transportation	☐	☐	☐
Close to Schools / Daycare	☐	☐	☐
Close to Places of Worship	☐	☐	☐
Near Recreational Facilities	☐	☐	☐
Close to Airport	☐	☐	☐
Near Police and Fire Department	☐	☐	☐

www.ingramcontent.com/pod-product-compliance
Lightning Source LLC
Chambersburg PA
CBHW071417210526
45465CB00001B/437